Tasos Leivaditis' Triptych

Tasos Leivaditis' Triptych

Battle at the Edge of the Night
This Star Is For All of Us
The Wind at the Crossroads of the World

Tasos Leivaditis

Translated by

N. N. Trakakis

ANTHEM PRESS

Anthem Press
An imprint of Wimbledon Publishing Company
www.anthempress.com

This edition first published in UK and USA 2022
by ANTHEM PRESS
75–76 Blackfriars Road, London SE1 8HA, UK
or PO Box 9779, London SW19 7ZG, UK
and
244 Madison Ave #116, New York, NY 10016, USA

British Library Cataloguing-in-Publication Data
A catalogue record for this book is available from the British Library.

Library of Congress Cataloging-in-Publication Data
Names: Leivaditēs, Tasos, author. | Trakakis, Nick, editor.
Title: Tasos Leivaditis' triptych : Battle at the edge of the night,
This star is for all of us, The wind at the crossroads of the world /
Tasos Leivaditis; translated by N.N. Trakakis.
Other titles: Triptych Description: London; New York, NY : Anthem Press, 2022. |
Includes bibliographical references. |
Identifiers: LCCN 2022000084 | ISBN 9781785278822 (paperback) |
ISBN 9781785278839 (pdf) | ISBN 9781785278846 (epub)
Subjects: LCSH: Leivaditēs, Tasos–Translations into English. | LCGFT: Poetry.
Classification: LCC PA5623.E5 T37 2022 | DDC 889.1/34–dc23/eng/20220107
LC record available at https://lccn.loc.gov/2022000084

ISBN-13: 978-1-78527-882-2 (Pbk)
ISBN-10: 1-78527-882-7 (Pbk)

Cover image: Tasos Leivaditis on Ai Stratis, c.1951 © Stylianos-Petros Halas

This title is also available as an e-book.

CONTENTS

TRANSLATOR'S NOTE

The Greek text upon which this translation is based can be found in the latest edition of Leivaditis' Collected Works, specifically Τάσος Λειβαδίτης, *Ποίηση, τόμος πρώτος: 1950–1966*, Athens: Metronomos Publications, 2015, pp. 13–102.

I am grateful to Dr Konstantina Georganta for her expert assistance with the translation. I also gratefully acknowledge Stylianos-Petros Halas, Leivaditis' literary executor, who granted permission for the publication of the translation. An earlier version of my translation of *This Star Is For All Of Us* was published in *Modern Greek Studies (Australia & New Zealand)*, vol. 18, 2016–17, pp. 291–308, and I thank the journal's editor, Professor Vrasidas Karalis, for permission to reuse this material. In my translation of *The Wind at the Crossroads of the World* I was aided by an earlier translation published by Nicholas Samaras in *Luna: A Journal of Poetry and Translation*, vol. 1, no. 1, Spring/Summer 1998, pp. 127–41.

Finally I thank Alma Lukic, librarian at Australian Catholic University, for helping to source many invaluable articles and books; and the staff at Anthem Press, for their assistance and expertise in the production and publication of the work.

INTRODUCTION

Tasos Leivaditis came to prominence in 1952–53 with his first three poetry books, presented here in translation as a 'triptych', seeing as all three arose from and address similar experiences in war-ravaged Greece. By this time Leivaditis' youth was over (he was 30 years of age when the first of the three books came out in 1952), and any inexperience or naïveté was also long gone, driven away by the winds of terror and torture which scarred the bodies (both physical and literary) of all leftist intellectuals of that generation. After the publication of his third book, in late 1952, Leivaditis was hailed by the left, in both Greece and abroad, as one of the greatest new talents to have appeared in recent years, and at the same time he was being persecuted and imprisoned by the police state – a polarity in the reception of Leivaditis' work that mirrored the deep divisions in Greece and Europe at large in the early Cold War years.

While the Cold War is only of historical interest today, Leivaditis' triptych continues to be widely read and loved: it is not unusual for lines or passages to be recited by heart, or set to music in popular festivals, or spraypainted on walls in Athens. Even commentators and critics, until fairly recently, tended to concentrate on Leivaditis' early and more 'political' writings, commonly drawing a sharp line between these writings and those that followed after Leivaditis' so-called political deconversion. But if we are to better understand Leivaditis' early work, and in particular his first three works, we need to delve into the context, both biographical and sociohistorical, out of which they emerged. This is what I shall attempt here, beginning with the bright and youthful Leivaditis and his relatively unknown first forays into the world of letters.

Days of Youth

Leivaditis was born in Athens on 20 April 1922, on the eve of Easter Sunday, which is in part why he was given the name 'Tasos' (short for 'Anastasios', derived from the Greek word for 'resurrection').[1] Tasos, the youngest of four

---

1. I say 'in part' because, according to his daughter, his premature birth nearly cost him his life, and so 'Anastasios' seemed a fitting name for one who was practically saved from

siblings (a sister, two brothers and a stepbrother), was nicknamed 'Byron' and 'Leopardi' at school and seemed destined for the life of a brooding poet, while his taller and eldest brother Alekos turned to acting, becoming a popular performer on the screen and stage, especially in light musical and comedic roles. Another brother, Mimis, worked as a musician in the Greek National Opera. Music, indeed, played an important part in all the brothers' upbringing: all were taught piano and violin, and in later life Tasos would write his poems each morning to the accompaniment of classical music.

In this cultured and relatively affluent family environment (the father, Lysandros, had become a prosperous textile merchant in Athens, after having moved there at the turn of the century from a village in the province of Arcadia in the Peloponnese), Tasos enjoyed a happy and carefree childhood, adored by friends and family alike, above all by his mother (Vasilike Kontopoulos), who indulged her youngest child's every whim – and would be beautifully memorialized in return in many of that child's adult verses. But dark clouds would soon encroach upon this idyllic landscape of Leivaditis' youth. The first of these took the form of world war in the political sphere and poverty in the personal domain.

Despite his predilection for poetry, which he had been writing since 12 years of age, Leivaditis enrolled in the Law School of the University of Athens.[2] This was late summer 1940, when war in Europe was raging. Having overrun Belgium and the Netherlands, German forces rapidly advanced through the dense forests of the Ardennes, capturing Paris as well as Jean-Paul Sartre and Henri Cartier-Bresson, who were taken to war prisoners' camps in Germany. In early September, London became the first casualty of the Luftwaffe's devastating 'blitz', and the following month, on the fateful day of 28 October, Greece too entered the war. Ioannis Metaxas, leader of Greece's dictatorial regime since 1936, tried to maintain neutrality at the outbreak of the war, but his hand was forced once Mussolini demanded that the Italians be allowed to enter Greece. Metaxas' legendary refusal prompted an immediate Italian invasion, but nearly as quickly the Italian forces were pushed back across the Albanian border by the far smaller Greek contingent, commanded by General Alexander Papagos.

death. See Vaso Hala-Leivaditis, 'My Best Friend, In the End ...', in *To Dendro* [Greek], no. 171–72, Autumn 2009, p. 132.

2. Yannis Kouvaras places Leivaditis' university entrance in 1940, while Apostolos Benatsis places it in 1943 and adds that Leivaditis dropped out of university after about a year. See Kouvaras, 'Leivaditis Chronology', *Diavazo* [Greek], no. 228, 13 December 1989, p. 20; Benatsis, *Tasos Leivaditis' Poetic Mythology* [Greek] (Athens: Epikairotita, 1991), p. 53. But if, as Kouvaras states (and as seems likely for someone born in 1922), Leivaditis began his secondary school studies in 1934, then it is more likely that he began his university studies in 1940 than in 1943.

What the Italians could not manage, the Germans swiftly accomplished. On 6 April 1941, Germany invaded both Yugoslavia and Greece. By the end of the month, the Wehrmacht had entered Athens and raised the swastika on the Acropolis. Metaxas did not live to see this ignominious defeat, having died in January and been replaced by one of his ministers, Alexandros Koryzis. But as the German troops marched towards Athens, Koryzis opted for suicide rather than surrender. Emmanuel Tsouderos, a Cretan banker, took up the reins and fled to his home island, along with his ministers and king (George II), before the Germans arrived in the capital. But even Crete would be captured in the following month, forcing the king and government to withdraw to Alexandria, Egypt. By June 1941, the whole of Greece was under a tripartite occupation, consisting of German, Italian and Bulgarian forces. Helped in no small measure by an anti-communist collaborationist Greek government, the occupying forces would unleash a wave of brutal violence upon the population, including disproportionate and indiscriminate reprisals involving mass arrests and executions, and even the destruction of whole villages.

Destitution and death were everywhere, in Athens especially. During the first winter of the Occupation, in 1941–42, an apocalyptic famine swept through the city. According to Roderick Beaton, 'as many as forty thousand civilians may have died from starvation in Athens and Piraeus alone. Between 1941 and 1943, the victims of famine are estimated to have reached a quarter of a million'.[3] Leivaditis' own household was not spared: as a result of the war, his father's textile business went bankrupt and in 1943 his father died. That was also the year when Leivaditis abandoned his studies and joined the resistance, inaugurating his active political engagement.

The Resistance

Leivaditis' interest in communism was sparked in his early teens, although he did not grow up in a leftist family. His childhood friend Nikos Drettas recounts that

> We were introduced to Marxism by two boys, who were brothers from a nearby bourgeois family. On their own accord they had rented a small room with a bookcase. They brought along as many books on Marxism as they could, we too brought our own, and gradually the initiation began. We then entered into a new world: we discovered that we were living in a place without light and, opening ourselves up to the Marxist

---

3. Roderick Beaton, *Greece: Biography of a Modern Nation* (London: Allen Lane, 2019), p. 274.

perspective, we noticed a different side to things, we realized that there could be a more honourable and just society.[4]

This fledgling communist cell was shut down by the Metaxas regime when it came to power in August 1936. In February 1941, Drettas, but not Leivaditis (who was one year younger), was called up for military service. A year later, after being discharged, Drettas decided to flee the country along with Leivaditis and another school friend Kostas Kotzias (who later co-wrote two screenplays with Leivaditis[5]). As Drettas tells the story, they left in February of 1942 with fake IDs, claiming that they were residents of Samos (an Aegean island off the coast of western Turkey), but when they got there they were arrested by the Italians and thrown into a filthy and overcrowded jail.[6] This was to be Leivaditis' first in a series of imprisonments. It was also to be, according to Drettas, the beginning of a transformation in Leivaditis' character: 'He started to become more secretive. Later he confided that his secretiveness was a bulwark against the responsibility he felt towards his fellow man, and he often repeated the phrase, "only others exist and our life with them." No, don't assume that Tasos was withdrawn. His secretiveness had the power to stir him up'.[7]

It was this sense of solidarity that led Leivaditis, as well as his brother Alekos and their sister Chrysaphenia, to join the Resistance – more specifically, the resistance movement known as the National Liberation Front (Εθνικό Απελευθερωτικό Μέτωπο, ΕΑΜ), which was founded in September 1941 by the Communist Party of Greece (Κομμουνιστικό Κόμμα Ελλάδας, ΚΚΕ) in conjunction with other left-wing and left-of-centre parties. Several other resistance groups were established during the Axis Occupation, the most significant of these being the National Republican Greek League (Εθνικός Δημοκρατικός Ελληνικός Σύνδεσμος, EDES), but they rarely cooperated with one another, and none had the appeal, size and power of EAM. Despite the influence of the Communist Party upon EAM, the latter was never a mere subsidiary of the former: EAM developed a broad base of support, recruiting members from diverse social strata and ideological backgrounds, including non-communists

4. Quoted in Vasilis Zilakos and Yiorgos Chronas, 'A Portrait of Leivaditis by His Friend, Nikos Drettas', *Odos Panos* [Greek], no. 140, April–June 2008, p. 50.
5. One of these was for the now-classic film, Συνοικία το Όνειρο ('Suburb of Dreams', 1961, directed by Alekos Alexandrakis), which caused an uproar at the time for its realistic portrayal of the slums of Athens. At the premiere, the police shut down the building's electricity and forced the audience to evacuate; in the ensuing scuffle, Tasos Leivaditis' brother, the actor Alekos, was arrested but later released. The film was banned and was eventually permitted to screen only in heavily censored form.
6. See Zilakos and Chronas, 'A Portrait of Leivaditis', pp. 50–51.
7. Quoted in Zilakos and Chronas, 'A Portrait of Leivaditis', p. 51.

and church leaders. EAM was particularly popular amongst the youth, and it was the youth wing of the movement, known as the United Panhellenic Organization of Youth (Ενιαία Πανελλαδική Οργάνωση Νέων, EPON) that Leivaditis joined soon after its formation in February 1943.

At EPON's offices and functions Leivaditis would get to meet some of the best and brightest leftist intellectuals and artists of his time. One of these was the now celebrated composer, Mikis Theodorakis, who had arrived in Athens in July 1943 after graduating from high school in Tripoli (the capital of Leivaditis' father's homeland, Arcadia). Theodorakis and Leivaditis would not meet till late in 1944, after the liberation; and in later years, from 1960 onwards, they would establish an acclaimed songwriting collaboration.

In February 1943, as the youth of Athens began signing up to EPON, the country lost its leading poet, Kostis Palamas. Attended by up to 100,000 people, the funeral turned into a massive rally against the occupiers, as another of Greece's great poets, Angelos Sikelianos, placed his hands on the coffin and exclaimed:

On this casket rests all of Greece!
[...] Awesome flags of freedom unfold in the air!

The funeral ended with the defiant crowd singing the outlawed Greek national anthem. The repression and violence, however, continued unabated: the new collaborationist government of Ioannis Rallis (installed in April of 1943) oversaw the systematic arrest and deportation of Greek Jews (by August, virtually all of Greece's Jews had been sent to their death) as well as the formation of the feared Security Batallions (Τάγματα Ασφαλείας), a military force armed by the Germans that would hunt down EAM resistance fighters.

Worse still, a civil war broke out between the military arm of EAM, known as the National Popular Liberation Army (Ελληνικός Λαϊκός Απελευθερωτικός Στρατός, ELAS), and its main rival, EDES. Sporadic clashes at the beginning of 1943 became increasingly more violent as the year wore on, with EAM-ELAS fearing that its role in any post-liberation government would be severely curtailed by the smaller but British-backed EDES, and EDES in its turn concerned about a communist takeover. This was not the first time Greeks had turned against one another while fighting a foreign enemy: at the very origins of the modern Greek nation-state, in 1823–24, a fratricidal battle between the rival governments of Theodoros Kolokotronis and Georgios Kountouriotis took place during the war of independence against the Ottomans. Internal conflicts continued to mark Greek society in the first half of the twentieth century, with the 'National Schism' – the divide between republicans (or 'Venizelists', represented by Eleftherios Venizelos' Liberal Party) and royalists (represented by the Populists or People's Party, led by Dimitrios Gounaris and Panayiotis Tsaldaris) – seen by many as prefiguring the internecine warfare between left and right during and after World War II.

A truce between ELAS and EDES in February 1944 and the retreat and defeat of the Nazi armies in Europe (epitomized by the Normandy invasion in June and the liberation of Paris in August) bode well for Greece. On 12 October the German troops withdrew from Athens; a few days later British forces reached the capital and were enthusiastically received by the Athenians; and on 18 October the exiled Greek government returned, now led by George Papandreou, a staunch anti-communist. As John Iatrides and Linda Wrigley explain, in their edited volume on the civil war, the leading factions in Greece were now faced with momentous decisions:

> In the fall of 1944, at the moment of liberation from the German occu-
> piers, Greece stood 'at the crossroads' and in need of a new constitu-
> tional and social order. At least in principle, the political paths open
> before the populace ranged across the entire ideological compass: from a
> dictatorship of the Left or the Right to a moderate socialist, progressive
> democratic, or rigidly conservative regime; from a republican to a mon-
> archist form of government. The final choice could have been made on
> the basis of a passionate but peaceful electoral contest to determine the
> nation's will. But the factions that vied for influence over the state pro-
> moted their particular agendas with a vehemence, exclusiveness, and
> mistrust that destroyed any chance for genuine compromise and rec-
> onciliation. Before long the political tug of war turned into full-scale
> civil war.[8]

The opportunity for repairing and rejuvenating a country in ruins was lost and overtaken by a traumatic adventure indelibly burned in the lives and mem-ories of an entire generation, including Leivaditis and Theodorakis.

The *Dekemvriana*

By December of 1944, Papandreou's coalition government was rent apart by disputes between left and right over the composition and leadership of the new national army and the disarmament of resistance groups. EAM-ELAS con-trolled about two-thirds of the country at the time of liberation, and so they expected a proportionate role in any newly formed army. When Papandreou

---

8. John O. Iatrides and Linda Wrigley (eds), *Greece at the Crossroads: The Civil War and Its Legacy* (University Park: Pennsylvania State University Press, 1995), pp. vii–viii.

and his British backers refused this, demanding instead that ELAS disarm and demobilize, the EAM ministers resigned from the coalition and called for a mass demonstration to be held the next day, Sunday, 3 December. A huge number of people descended upon Constitution Square in the centre of the capital (some put the number at 60,000, others as high as 250,000), and chaos was suddenly unleashed when the police, unprovoked by the unarmed and peaceful protestors, opened fire. A number of people were killed (estimates vary from a minimum of 7 to a maximum of 28) and many more were wounded. Theodorakis, at the forefront of this Bloody Sunday, recounts:

> Police were shooting in cold blood. It was horrible. This time, they shot directly into the crowd. Hundreds were wounded; the dead lay all over the place. The pavements became red with blood. It was the first time I ever saw so much blood. I grabbed a Greek flag. I soaked it in the blood and stood up again.[9]

Another of Leivaditis' close friends, Titos Patrikios (who went on to become a prominent post-war poet[10]), has similarly stated:

> I can still see it very clearly, I have not forgotten […] The Athens police firing on the crowd from the roof of the parliament in Syntagma Square. The young men and women lying in pools of blood, everyone rushing down the stairs in total shock, total panic.[11]

Patrikios, who was then only sixteen, recounts that he 'jumped up on the fountain in the middle of the square, the one that is still there, and I began to shout: "Comrades, don't disperse! Victory will be ours! Don't leave. The time has come. We will win!"'[12] Over the course of December (hence the name of 'Dekemvriana'), heavy fighting broke out between ELAS and government units, the latter assisted and protected by British troops and even aerial bombers. By early January, ELAS had been forced to give up the capital; thousands had been killed, and many thousands more had been rounded up by the British

---

9. Quoted in George Giannaris, *Mikis Theodorakis: Music and Social Change* (New York: Praeger Publishers, 1972), pp. 39–40.
10. For an English anthology of Patrikios' poetry, see *The Lions' Gate: Selected Poems of Titos Patrikios*, trans. Christopher Bakken and Roula Konsolaki (Kirksville: Truman State University Press, 2006).
11. Quoted in Ed Vuillamy and Helena Smith, 'Athens 1944: Britain's Dirty Secret', *The Guardian*, 30 November 2014: https://www.theguardian.com/world/2014/nov/30/athens-1944-britains-dirty-secret.
12. Quoted in Vuillamy and Smith, 'Athens 1944'.

and sent to camps in the Middle East. Retreating ELAS bands, in retaliation, took thousands of civilian hostages from the neighbourhoods of Athens, herding them north, beating and killing many along the way. Such 'red terror' only fuelled the subsequent campaign of 'white terror', one of whose victims was Leivaditis.

From Chatzikosta to Varkiza

Leivaditis was arrested for participating in the *Dekemvriana* and sent to prison, along with many others who had (or were suspected of having) taken part. The prison, in Leivaditis' case, was Chatzikosta (Φυλακές Χατζηκώστα), a building initially used, from 1856, as an orphanage funded by a bequest from Yiorgos Chatzikonstas and his wife Katerina.[13] During the war, the building was converted into a prison by the collaborationist government and was run by the notorious Special Security Service (Ειδική Ασφάλεια), an arm of the SS which targeted not only communists but all resistance fighters.

The squalid basement cells of Chatzikosta would often be the last place of residence for inmates before facing the firing squad, as is movingly testified by Nikolaos Tzouyanatos' recently republished *Όταν οι τοίχοι μιλούν* (When Walls Talk). Tzouyanatos (1906–94) studied philology at the University of Athens, specializing in ancient Greek and Latin, and went on teach at the distinguished Varvakeio school in 1943. But following the *Dekemvriana* he found himself (unjustly) charged with accessory to murder and was imprisoned at Chatzikosta for five months (5 March–4 August 1945). While there, he transcribed the messages written on the walls by those condemned to death (soon to be executed by the Germans, usually after having been betrayed by Greek collaborators); he then published these last testaments in a series of newspaper articles in October 1945. In later years, in a previously unpublished prologue to these articles, he wrote:

> The war [i.e. WW II] was over, but the tragic and bloody conflicts continued. Honourable and courageous fighters, who risked their life against the violence of the occupiers, found themselves under ruthless persecution. It made no difference whether you were a communist or not. It was irrelevant whether you fulfilled your prescribed duty towards

---

13. It is therefore thought that the name of the prison was derived from the orphanage's benefactors, though it was possibly also named after the director of the prison during the Occupation, coincidentally surnamed Chatzikostas (but without the 'n'). The orphanage continues to operate to this day, though in a different location; see http://xatzikonsta.gr/.

the nation and your fellow citizen. For the postwar state, which in many cases was made of up collaborators and sycophants of the occupying powers, you were an outcast, a heinous monster! You had to be chased down, starved, wiped out![14]

After more than a month in prison, Leivaditis was released following the Varkiza Agreement on 12 February 1945. This peace treaty, signed by the warring factions at the Athenian seaside suburb of Varkiza, provided an amnesty for the defeated ELAS fighters, who were required in exchange to disband and surrender their arms within two weeks. ELAS, now disarmed, was easy prey for the ruthless Right, which seized control of the security and state apparatus. As Beaton has said, 'For many on the left, ever since, "Varkiza" has been remembered, regretted and deplored as an unforgivable act of surrender by the communist leadership at a time when EAM and ELAS still held most of Greece under their control.'[15]

In Love and in Print

In 1945 Leivaditis found freedom, after Chatzikosta, but also love, after meeting Maria Stoupas.[16] Maria was to inspire many of his poems, including *This Star Is For All Of Us*, as well as supporting him through her seamstress work when Leivaditis would be virtually unemployable due to his leftist history (as happened when the junta took power in 1967 and Leivaditis lost his job at a newspaper). They married in 1946, and had only one child, a daughter Vaso. But Tasos, invariably stylishly dressed and often described as handsome and incurably romantic, had several other women in his life as well, and it's hard to believe that this was completely unknown to Maria. Titos Patrikios, Leivaditis' poet-friend whom I quoted earlier, has disclosed:

---

14. Nikolaos Tzouyanatos, *When Walls Talk: A Chronicle of the Basement Cells of Chatzikosta Prison (October 1945)* [Greek] (Athens: Hestia Bookshop, 2020), p. 21.
15. Beaton, *Greece*, pp. 295–96.
16. There is some disagreement about how well, if at all, Leivaditis and Stoupas knew one another prior to 1945. Their daughter states that 'in 1945 he [Tasos Leivaditis] met my mother, Maria Stoupas', and adds that the two lived in the same neighbourhood of Athens (the implication being, in light of the quoted passage, that they had not formed any relationship before 1945 even though they had grown up and lived in close proximity) (Vaso Hala-Leivaditis, 'My Best Friend', p. 133). This is contradicted by Kouvaras ('Leivaditis Chronology', pp. 20–21), who states that the two had known one another since childhood, and that after Maria lost her father during the Occupation, Tasos would ask her each time they crossed paths: 'When, Maria, will you take off your black [mourning] clothes so that we can marry?'

Leivaditis had many affairs. It wasn't possible for him to meet a woman and not try to seduce her, not try to besiege her, sometimes even forcefully. As he trusted my friendship and discretion, he told me about many of his erotic adventures; these gave him great pleasure, but more often disappointment, dramatic rifts and guilt would pile up. Other affairs were over even before they had begun, in a comically anodyne way. But all of them ended up in his poetry, this constituting his sole commitment.[17]

At the age of 24, in 1946, Leivaditis published his very first poems, the first entitled 'Το τραγούδι του Χατζηδημήτρη (απόσπασμα)' (The Song of Hadjidimitri (excerpt)) in the November issue of the journal *Elefthera Grammata* (*Ελεύθερα Γράμματα*); and this was quickly followed by 'Απ' το Δεκέμβρη' (From December), in the December issue of the same journal.[18] The recently established *Elefthera Grammata*, founded in May 1945 by Dimitris Photiades, was to become a well-respected literary journal of the Left in its short life-span (it ceased circulation in March 1951). Its editorial board included writers of the calibre of Nikephoros Vrettakos (as well as Stratis Doukas, who was to testify in support of Leivaditis during the latter's trial), and contributors included a range of leading leftist intellectuals (such as Kostas Varnalis, Tasos Vournas, Markos Avgheris and Yannis Ritsos). The journal's progressive leanings made it an obvious target of the Right, but also of the KKE, as was unfortunately illustrated by Vrettakos' defence of pacifism in *Δυο άνθρωποι μιλούν για την ειρήνη του κόσμου* (Two Men Talk About World Peace, 1949). In the words of one scholar, 'This book of peace thrust Vrettakos into a violent war. A right-wing gang tried to kill him on the street, while from the Left came the ominous message: "The Communist Party has decided to execute you".'[19] Although not executed, he was excommunicated from the party, which also had him banished from the journal's board. In years to come, such bullying behaviour would become a regular feature of life in the literary Left, with many of Leivaditis' colleagues (and eventually Leivaditis himself) falling foul of the party.[20]

---

17. Titos Patrikios, 'One More Visit to Leivaditis', *To Dendro* [Greek], no. 171–72, Autumn 2009, p. 101.
18. Tasos Leivaditis, 'The Song of Hadjidimitri (excerpt)', *Elefthera Grammata* [Greek], no. 55, 15 November 1946, p. 339; and 'From December', *Elefthera Grammata*, no. 57, 15 December 1946, p. 369.
19. Angela Kastrinakis, *Literature in the 1940s Decade* [Greek] (Athens: Association of Greek Academic Libraries, 2015), pp. 159–60.
20. Leivaditis' later work, from 1957 onwards, was often criticized for its 'deviations' from the orthodox party line. Also, when the KKE split in 1968 into an 'external' pro-Soviet

'The Song of Hadjidimitri', placed in the 'New Poets' column of *Elefthera Grammata*, is unlike anything Leivaditis was to include in his Collected Works. Inspired by the rugged landscape and heroic traditions of Crete, and its recent valiant battle against the Germans in May 1941, Leivaditis opens with the following portrait of Hadjidimitri the *palikari* (a brave and gallant young man):

Riding horseback as a child on Psiloritis[21]
he'd beckon the dawn to appear and take the sun for a stroll
feeding his dreams to eagles
loosening in the distance white sheets of clouds in a dream
and that song of his in the wind
taken up by Chelmos,[22] let go by Olympus[23]
then from summit to cloud completed by angels.
Other times he'd leap at dawn from the waters
dancing the pentozali[24] on chestnut-coloured shores
shoulder to shoulder with wind and sea.
Hey great lad, Hadji-Dimitri!
Your breasts were citadels along Crete's coasts
and your breath each morning sent a fragrant scent upon the flowers.

On exhibit here, from the outset, is Leivaditis' ability to concisely create a captivating tempo and mood, in this instance one that is vibrant and vigorous, as well as ebullient, if not euphoric. But what is unusual, in comparison with the poetry for which Leivaditis was to become renowned, is the folkloric setting, as signalled by Psiloritis, the *palikari* and the pentozali dance. More unusual still is the harmonious, indeed otherworldly, bond between the human and natural environments: having instructed the dawn to appear, Hadjidimitri takes the sun for a walk and feeds his dreams to the eagles. The wind, moreover, is portrayed as a bright, benevolent force joyfully dancing with the sea and carrying the hero's song from mountain tops to the angels in the heavens – images to keep

---

faction and an 'internal' Euro-communist one, Leivaditis sided with the latter and encountered strong criticism for doing so.

21. *Psiloritis:* a mountainous range or massif in the centre of Crete, whose highest peak (known as Mt Ida) reaches 2,456 m.

22. *Chelmos* (Χελμός): also known as Aroania (Αροάνια), a mountain range in Achaea, northern Peloponnese. Its tallest peak reaches an altitude of 2,355 m.

23. *Olympus:* the highest mountain in Greece (2,918 m), on the border of Macedonia and Thessaly, and the famous home of the 12 principal Greek gods.

24. *Pentozali:* a traditional Cretan dance, vigorous and lively, involving high jumping movements, with the dancers holding each other by the shoulders and moving at a progressively faster pace.

in mind when we turn to depictions of the wind, and of nature at large, in the triptych.

Leivaditis' next poem, 'From December', commemorates the Resistance and the *Dekemvriana*, precisely two years after the latter event. The style and setting are again demotic and folkloric, but now the *palikaria* are *andartes* (rebels, partisans) fighting for socialist ideals:

> the *syrtos*[25] of war has begun
> headed by a handkerchief as red as our blood
> – lads we salute you! –
> pulled along by sun-born Freedom herself

With their distinctive gallantry (*leventia*), these young lads swoop down like hawks on Athens:

> Standing tall like Olympus
> the Gorgopotamos[26] at their feet
> from their torn uniforms
> sprout forests of fir trees
> and a hawk with open wings, pouncing fiercely

The poem, however, concludes with the foreboding sense that the battle, though not necessarily the war overall, is doomed:

> And if our bullets are all used up
> we fill our rifles with justice and rage.
> And if we all fall, still we are many
> the dance continues well through the age.

In his subsequent offering, Leivaditis continued with politically engaged poetry, this time translating a poem from the French, Loys Masson's 'Épitaphe' (rendered as 'Ἐπιτάφιος', Funeral Hymn).[27] The Mauritian-born Masson

---

25. *Syrtos:* a popular Greek folk dance with ancient origins, where the dancers link hands in a chain headed by a leader who often breaks away from the basic steps of the group and improvises while flourishing his handkerchief.

26. *Gorgopotamos:* river in central Greece, now famous as the site where the two warring sides of the civil war, in a rare show of unity against the occupying German army, joined forces on the night of 24–25 November 1942 to blow up the Gorgopotamos railway viaduct linking Thessaloniki and Athens.

27. Loys Masson's poem was published in his collection, *La Lumière Naît Le Mercredi* (Paris: Éditions Pierre Seghers, 1946), pp. 65–66.

(1915–69) left for Paris in 1939 and spent the occupation years in Villeneuve-lès-Avignon, working as an editor for *Poésie* (which would become the mouth-piece of Resistance poetry during the war) and taking an active part in underground activity. He is said to have combined 'a robust and unorthodox Catholic faith with an equally energetic and unconventional Communist fervour'.[28] This is evident in the poem translated by Leivaditis, where religious and political imagery (Easter, comradeship, justice, freedom) are seamlessly woven together, in celebration of those who fought and fell in the French Resistance:

> I saw you giving a helping hand to the dream
> > so that the splendour of the stars might shimmer from afar.
> If a war were ever just, it would be this one.

The last line is repeated later in the poem, and Leivaditis would no doubt extend the sentiment expressed there as well as in the hymn's conclusion to the leftist rebels and resistance fighters of Greece:

> If I speak of a garden, it is about your hearts
> > where beneath freedom's rosarium
> you, my brothers, taught us
> > the mournful language of roses.

Leivaditis' translation was published in the September 1947 issue of the periodical *Themelio* (Θεμέλιο).[29] The periodical lasted only two issues (both published in 1947), but was notable for facilitating the rise of a new breed of leftist writers who had come together in the premises of EPON under the leadership of Ritsos and the direction of Dimitris Despotidis, the head of the EPON Athens branch.[30] This group of enthusiastic and promising young

---

28. Michael Kelly, 'Catholicism and the Left in Twentieth-Century France', in Kay Chadwick (ed.), *Catholicism, Politics and Society in Twentieth-Century France* (Liverpool: Liverpool University Press, 2000), p. 154. Masson's attempt at reconciling Catholicism and Communism occurred at a time when this was expressly forbidden by the Vatican. In a decree dated 1 July 1949 and approved by Pope Pius XII, the Vatican declared Catholics who professed Communist doctrine to be excommunicated as apostates from the Christian faith.
29. See *Themelio* [Greek], no. 2, September 1947, p. 32. On the next page (p. 33) was published a (translated) letter by Masson, expressing his support for and solidarity with the editors of the journal and the Greek people more broadly.
30. Despotidis relaunched 'Themelio' in 1963 as a publishing house, which continues to publish leading leftist writers.

writers was known as 'Θεμέλιο' (*themelio*, foundation, bedrock) and included Leivaditis, Kotzias and Patrikios, as well as others who went on to become established figures in the post-war cultural left, such as the critic and historian Alexandros Argyriou and the poet and painter Mihalis Katsaros.[31] The journal they produced, *Themelio*, was subtitled 'Ομάδα Νέων Λογοτεχνών', Society of Young Writers. Formed in 1945, the Society had grown to a significant size by 1947, holding readings and meetings between older and younger generations, but by mid-1948 the group was disbanded, when (as we'll see shortly) many of its members were exiled to prison camps or called up for military service. The seeds nonetheless were sown, and would flower in the difficult years to follow.[32]

Having participated in the leftist literary ventures of *Elefthera Grammata* and *Themelio*, Leivaditis seemingly makes an about-turn by contributing to *Nea Hestia* (*Νέα Εστία*) – one of Greece's most prestigious and longest running literary journals, founded in 1927 by the prolific and influential writer Gregorios Xenopoulos (1867–1951). Xenopoulos may have had leftist sympathies, becoming for a time an advocate of Platon Drakoulis (1858–1934), a socialist thinker who translated Kropotkin, taught at Oxford and was briefly elected to parliament. But neither Drakoumis nor Xenopoulos aligned themselves with communism, and the same applies to *Nea Hestia*. In its long history, the journal has distanced itself from the political left, seeking instead either ideological neutrality or favouring the sort of liberal cosmopolitanism that would appeal to urban, pro-western professionals. And so, when Leivaditis publishes 'Η κυρά της Όστριας' (The Lady of Ostro) in an August 1947 issue of *Nea Hestia*, his twelve-stanza poem taking up nearly two whole pages,[33] his friends in the Society of Young Writers would naturally be bemused.[34]

---

31. On this group of young writers and their desire to launch a new journal, despite KKE's reservations, see Dimitris Raftopoulos, *Aris Alexandrou: The Exile*, 2nd ed. [Greek] (Athens: Sokolis Publications, 2004), p. 151.

32. Both issues of *Themelio* were republished as an appendix to Phyllis Mitsou's collection of short stories, *Διηγήματα της εφηβείας και του πολέμου* (Stories of Youth and War, published in Athens by Kastaniotis; no date provided, but possibly 1980 as per note on p. 151), which is dedicated to 'the 1945 Society of Young Writers.' Mitsou was part of the editorial committee of *Themelio*, and went on to practice law in Athens.

33. Leivaditis, 'The Lady of Ostro', *Nea Hestia* [Greek], vol. 42, no. 482, 1 August 1947, pp. 917–18.

34. This is not to say that *Nea Hestia* in the post-war period refused to publish leftist writers. Indeed, a glance at the issues of the journal around the time when Leivaditis' poem appeared (1 August 1947) will reveal translations of poems, short stories and essays by major French leftists such as Aragon, Sartre, Camus and Eluard, as well as reviews of books by leftist Greek writers such as Vrettakos and Katsaros (this, however, seems to exhaust the presence of the Greek left in the pages of the journal at that time).

Like his earlier poems, Leivaditis makes extensive use here of the forms and motifs of the traditional demotic song, which (as critics have noted) experienced a revival during the Occupation, as writers sought to reconnect with the national literary traditions originating from the nineteenth-century revolution. As with the 'Song of Hadjidimitri', a cheerful, even ecstatic, mood is created in 'The Lady of Ostro', which charts the movements of the southerly Mediterranean wind, called 'Ostro' (Greek: Όστρια), a warm and humid wind often carrying rain. In ancient Greek mythology it was deified as *Notos* (Latin *Auster*), the fearful god who brought on the desiccating hot winds of late summer which would burn the crops. In Leivaditis' poem, Ostro has none of these destructive qualities, but is personified as an enchanting, lissom lady (even as a 'mermaid Panagia'[35]), in carefree communion with the wildlife around her, passionately pursued by other winds and young sailors, and all this set against the azure sky and sea, wind-borne kisses from Kalymnos, the music of a lovesick Monemvasiot violinist or of a child playing a lute made from dolphin bones while birds and bees fly in and out of his breeches! It is a marvellous poem, well summarized by Yiorgos Balourdos as

> featuring vivid surrealist elements, without compromising the symbols of the folk tradition; exquisite adjectives; a religious sense of earth-bound metaphysical beauty; words that shimmer in the Aegean sea; and aromatic imagery highly reminiscent of the early Odysseus Elytis. But also embodying a folk metaphysics, one that sublimates the condition of nature in a way that brings Yannis Ritsos to mind. This optimistic poem gives rise to a beauty of bright smiles, a sun-drenched and hopeful atmosphere, with words replete with light and love, giving no indication at all of the poet's subsequent career.[36]

It is well worth, then, reproducing the first half of the poem:

My sailors, as you passed by and headed south,
did you happen to see her playing on her crag with the seagulls?

On a loom of salt and flying fish
sea nymphs lay out our white sails

---

35. *Panagia:* a title of Mary, the mother of Jesus, commonly used in the Orthodox Church; literally means 'all-holy'. Later in the poem, Ostro is referred to as 'the Virgin Mary of the Mid-Seas' and 'Lady full of Grace'.
36. Yiorgos Balourdos, 'Leivaditis: An Endless Conversation with the Dead', *Odos Panos* [Greek], no. 140, April–June 2008, p. 78.

and a deck boy strolls about the waves
stirring the sea with salvos and apples.

Pursued by the westerly she was running on the sand
gathering the waves on her white apron
bring her to us, o sun, bring her to us, o northerly
as she travels astride dolphins in fields of seaweed
with thousands of seagulls behind her holding her skirt
with thousands of bream around her, as she smiles brightly.

Lady of our white sails, my mermaid Panagia.
Awake lady of Kalymnos,[37] awake with three bitter oranges
and give us your plaits so that we can hoist the sails
send us a kiss too that we might have a favourable wind.
Can't you hear the waves, tall and slender lady of the sea?
Can't you see the winds fighting over you?
Or the young sailors of the easterly sending you from faraway masts
skyward greetings with their white caps?

Songs of the sea squeezed in shells
secrets of the world found in a sea urchin
the wind swiftly unlaced the bodice of the peach tree
and she rushed towards the crags
chased by children with two clams of eros
and with a barrage of plums the sailors broke down her door.

And you, blond child, playing a lute made of dolphin bones
with a sprig of moon behind your ear
with birds and bees flying in and out of your blue breeches
and ah! your breast can't contain so much heart
bring her to us, o sun, bring her to us, o northerly
play, that the winds may bring birds and kisses from Kalymnos
play, my boy, and count the sailors who aren't here
bring her to us, o sun, bring her to us, o northerly
play, that the girls in Monemvasia[38] might hear
and cut off their plaits to tie up the boats.

---

37. *Kalymnos:* an island in the south-eastern Aegean Sea, close to the Turkish coast.
38. *Monemvasia:* a medieval castle town on the south-eastern coast of the Peloponnese; also
    the birthplace of Yannis Ritsos.

Civil War

The delightful, light-hearted tones of these verses stand in stark contrast to the dark and dreadful time during which they were written – arguably the darkest period in modern Greek history. This was the civil war, which had (as noted earlier) sporadically erupted during World War II and in the *Dekemvriana*, but was now to take on much wider and more devastating proportions. Political and economic instability, polarization and violence were all on the rise in the year following Varkiza, as the British installed one ineffective government after another, and the right-wing backlash of the 'White Terror' tore through the country. As Beaton has said, 'It was enough to be related, even distantly, to someone identified as a "communist," for you to be beaten up, arrested, imprisoned or even killed.'[39] Cities and villages became battlegrounds between (to use the state's preferred terms) the 'national-minded' patriots (εθνικόφρονες) and the 'bandits' or 'Bulgars' of the Left, the latter tortured and killed in the thousands by militias and paramilitaries, which were staffed by anti-communist extremists and former quislings, with the protection (if not assistance) of the British.[40] German collaborators were released from prisons, while communists were purged from all sectors of society and the leftist press suppressed (their offices vandalized, their papers removed from the stands, etc.), despite government assurances following Varkiza that the freedom of the press would be upheld.[41]

By this time, the 'Iron Curtain' had descended across the European continent, as Churchill famously said in a speech given in Fulton, Missouri, on 5 March 1946. And from early on Greece would serve as an arena, if not a proxy, for this broader battle between the East and the West.[42] A few weeks after Churchill's speech, a group of thirty ex-ELAS members attacked a police outpost in the village of Litochoro (located on the eastern slopes of Mt Olympus), firing the first shots in the third and most deadly and protracted phase of the civil war. This was on the eve of the general elections on 31 March 1946 (the first since 1936),

---

39. Beaton, *Greece*, p. 296.
40. The statistics are terrible: 'According to EAM, 31,632 people were tortured, 1,289 killed and 6,671 wounded in an orgy of violence that lasted from February 1945 to March 1946 [...] The true motives behind this purge included revenge, thirst for power and fanaticism.' (Spyridon Plakoudas, *The Greek Civil War: Strategy, Counterinsurgency and the Monarchy* (London: Bloomsbury, 2017), p. 21) 'From February to July 1945, 20,000 persons had been arrested, over 500 had been murdered, and 2,961 had been condemned to death.' (Neni Panourgiá, *Dangerous Citizens: The Greek Left and the Terror of the State* (New York: Fordham University Press, 2009), p. 80)
41. See Yiorgos Leondaritis, *The Journalism and Literature of the Left: In Search of the Lost Left* [Greek] (Athens: Agra Publications, 2014), pp. 96–103.
42. See Andre Gerolymatos, *An International Civil War: Greece 1943–1949* (Yale University Press, 2016), who sees the civil war in Greece as a proxy conflict between foreign powers, an 'international civil war'.

which the Left boycotted on the grounds that fair elections could not be assured under the violent conditions that gripped the country at the time. Victory for the monarchist Right was therefore a foregone conclusion, and the new government headed by Constantine Tsaldaris soon adopted the White Terror as official policy.

It was no surprise, then, that a full-scale civil war reopened in the winter of 1946–47, on the initiative of the KKE leadership and leftist insurgents who had taken to the mountains in the north. The communist-controlled Democratic Army of Greece (Δημοκρατικός Στρατός Ελλάδας, DSE), commanded by Markos Vaphiades, managed to control a wide area of northern Greece for a substantial period of time, despite receiving scant support from allies like the Soviet Union, and despite being heavily outnumbered by the British-trained National Army of Greece. But the tide would turn once the Truman Doctrine was announced (in March 1947) and the Marshall Plan put into effect: the United States took over the mantle of chief external patron from Britain and began pouring massive military and economic aid into Greece.

The persecution of leftists in the meanwhile escalated, with the opening of a network of island prison camps for 'suspect' soldiers and civilians. In late 1947, the communist press is outlawed, the police sweep through the towns of northern Greece in search of communists, while the military evacuate entire regions, forcibly removing villagers so as to 'drain the "sea" (the people) within which the "fish" (insurgents) swam'.[43] And when in December the insurgents form a Provisional Democratic Government (with Vaphiades as prime minister), the Athens government retaliates by instituting the infamous Emergency Law 509, which outlaws the KKE, EAM and its affiliates, and all 'Communist activity' is subjected to harsh punishment, including the death penalty.

The civil war too escalated, having spread by the late autumn of 1948 throughout much of the country, and northern Greece especially. But the DSE was now fighting a losing battle. With Papagos as commander-in-chief of an American-supplied National Army (supplied with, amongst other things, napalm bombs), the communists were driven back to two mountain ranges close to the frontiers with Albania and Yugoslavia: Vitsi and Grammos. After fierce battles on these mountains in August 1949, the communists were soundly defeated and fled across the border into Albania. The war was over, but the bitterness and cleavages were certainly not, and the country was left smouldering in ashes: an estimated 80,000 dead, many more escaping to communist countries in Eastern Europe, and some 700,000 displaced from their homes by the fighting.

---

43. Plakoudas, *The Greek Civil War*, p. 82, borrowing of course from Mao. Plakoudas notes (on pp. 81, 110) that these evacuations increased the number of internally displaced people from about 141,000 in June 1947 to 413,000 in November of the same year; and by May 1949 the number peaked at 705,000 – over 10 per cent of the total population, and 25 per cent of the population of northern Greece.

Island Prisons

The climate of fear and fanaticism during the civil war is illustrated well by the front-page headline of the Athens daily, *Ta Nea*, for 4 May 1948: 'This Morning 24 People Executed in Athens and 130 in the Provinces Charged for Crimes during the December Uprising.'[44] The following month Leivaditis too would fall victim to this state-sanctioned terror: in June 1948 he was arrested and, without ever being brought to trial, imprisoned in various island prison camps for over three years. These camps were spread through the Aegean islands, where more than 100,000 people from 1947 to 1958 were deported, detained and subjected to physical and psychological violence. It's worth remembering that Auschwitz and the other Nazi death camps had only recently been discovered and liberated, and that the camps in Greece were the first of their kind in 'free' post-war Europe. But no ideology has a monopoly on evil. The concentration camp – this characteristically modern form of mass incarceration and punishment of 'dangerous citizens', where the state functions as both the law and its transgression[45] – had progressed since its British origins in the Boer War to unprecedented extremes in the Nazi Holocaust and the Soviet Gulags. And it's still very much with us: think only of Guantánamo Bay, Australia's pioneering Pacific 'solution' for unwanted asylum-seekers (officially called 'illegal maritime arrivals'),[46] and the system of internment camps

---

44. Quoted in Dimitris Photiades, *Reminiscences*, vol. 2, 2nd ed. [Greek] (Athens: Kedros, 1985), p. 359.
45. I'm borrowing from the title of Neni Panourgiá's brilliant study of this phenomenon in its modern Greek manifestations, and her description of the Greek prison islands as existing 'in a space where, as Begoña Aretxaga has noted, "the State was both the law and its transgression." They were set up to receive the Left as the wake, the refuse, the dregs of humanity, as undesirable and "superfluous"' (Panourgiá, *Dangerous Citizens*, p. 91, where she is quoting Begoña Aretxaga (1960–2002), a Basque anthropologist known for her work on Northern Ireland, Basque country, and state violence). The Italian philosopher, Giorgio Agamben, similarly speaks of the concentration camp as a 'space of exception' where the rule of law is suspended and detainees reduced to 'bare life' (an inhuman form of life, excluded from the ethical and legal spheres). This state of exception, Agamben provocatively claims, has become the rule in the modern world, revealing 'the hidden matrix and *nomos* of the political space in which we are still living' (Agamben, *Homo Sacer: Sovereign Power and Bare Life*, trans. Daniel Heller-Roazen (Stanford: Stanford University Press, 1998 [originally published in Italian, 1995]), p. 166).
46. The best work to come out of Australia's offshore detention system is Behrouz Boochani's *No Friend But The Mountains: Writing From Manus Prison*, trans. Omid Tofighian (Sydney: Picador, 2018), a book secretly composed one text message at a time while its Kurdish author (fleeing persecution in Iran) was imprisoned on Manus Island, Papua New Guinea.

(officially called 're-education centres', just as the camps in Greece were called) in China's Xinjiang region, presently housing over one million Uyghurs and other Muslim ethnic minorities.

Leivaditis was initially sent to Moudros, a town on the island of Lemnos, in the northern part of the Aegean. He was soon joined by many other leftist intellectuals, including Aris Alexandrou and Yannis Ritsos, the latter beginning there his *Diaries of Exile* with its 'descriptions of harsh labor, beatings, and meager rations, not to mention the feeling of entrapment caused both by the inescapable fact of imprisonment and by the daily repetition of the same routine'.[47]

A year later, in the summer of 1949, Leivaditis was transferred to the dreaded isle of Makronisos, again with many other leftist comrades in tow, including Ritsos, who has reported: 'Makronisos, like hell, has no stories to tell. There is nothing to say about it'.[48] And yet, that hell would leave its indelible imprint on the work of both Ritsos and Leivaditis, as the triptych translated here testifies. Makronisos, elongated in shape (hence its name, literally meaning 'long island'), lies very close to the town of Lavrion on the east Attica coast, 'where, people say, with the right – or wrong – wind one could hear the screams of the men being tortured'.[49] The island, lashed from all sides by the wind, is well known for its harsh, rugged and barren landscape. For this reason, it has usually gone uninhabited, except when the authorities of the day have wished to use it as a place of 'internal exile' and 'rehabilitation' of 'dangerous' elements of the population, as happened during the civil war. The 'Organization of Makronisos Rehabilitation Centres' (Οργανισμός Αναμορφωτηρίων Μακρονήσου, OAM) fell under the jurisdiction of the Army General Staff, with the purpose initially of cleansing suspect soldiers and officers from the ranks, but later broadened to encompass the 're-education' of any leftist, even civilians, into the principles of nationalism and to obtain from them written declarations renouncing communism.[50] Makronisos' function, in short, was to crush and humiliate the Left.

---

47. Karen Emmerich, 'Introduction' to Yannis Ritsos, *Diaries of Exile*, trans. Karen Emmerich and Edmund Keeley (Brooklyn: Archipelago Books, 2013), p. x.
48. Quoted in Mikis Theodorakis, *Journals of Resistance*, trans. Graham Webb (London: Hart-Davis MacGibbon, 1973), p. 45.
49. Panourgiá, *Dangerous Citizens*, p. 95.
50. The fact that the army oversaw the detention of civilians reflects the great power it had accrued in Greek society. However, none of the army staff who ran the Makronisos prison complex was ever brought to justice. This is the basis of the low budget but excellent film drama, *Η Νύχτα τ' Αγ' Αντώνη – Μακρόνησος BX11* (Saint Anthony's Night – Makronisos BX11, 2018, directed by Thanasis Skroubelos), where a mock trial of a former Makronisos commander and torturer is conducted many years later on the island. Another highly recommended film on Makronisos is the documentary *Like*

The prison complex on Makronisos was structured along military lines into four large battalions along the west coast, the fourth of these (located on the northern tip of the island) reserved for civilians. But soon after Leivaditis' arrival, as the civil war came to an end and the focus of the island camps shifted from soldiers to civilians, the civilian detainees were moved to two newly established Special Rehabilitation Schools for Civilians (Ειδικά Στρατόπεδα Αναμορφώσεως Ιδιωτών, ESAI), each administered by a separate battalion. In November 1949, Leivaditis and Alexandrou, along with 7,000 other political exiles, were sent to the BETO-ESAI, that is, the Rehabilitation School run by the Second Battalion (Β´ Ειδικό Τάγμα Οπλιτών, BETO).[51] There Leivaditis would come in contact with an impressive array of scholars, actors, musicians, directors, novelists and poets. The detainees' clandestine writings – concealed in crevices or in bottles buried in the earth, then passed on to visiting relatives to be smuggled out[52] – would go on to shape the course of post-war Greek literature and give rise to the genre of 'Makronisos poetry'.[53] In the apt words of one scholar, 'If, as Adorno said, there can be no poetry after Auschwitz, Makronisos proves otherwise.'[54]

These writings were a matter of survival and testimony, providing a witness to the outside world of the brutality of Makronisos, where the violence began as soon as one stepped upon the island's shores. New arrivals would be asked

---

Stone Lions At The Gateway Into Night (2012, directed by Olivier Zuchuat), which includes excerpts from Leivaditis' poetry.

51. See Raftopoulos, *Aris Alexandrou*, p. 167; Philippas Yeladopoulos, *Makronisos* [Greek] (Athens: [no publisher given], 1965), pp. 157–59; Kleovoulos A. Dendrinos, *Unknown Pages from Makronisos (1948–1950)* [Greek] (Athens: [no publisher given], 1998), pp. 43–45.

52. This indeed is how Leivaditis' first two poetry books secretly made their way out of Ai Stratis to Athens, with the help of his wife while visiting him in exile.

53. The creative output of the inmates also included church paintings and classical replicas – i.e. small-scale replicas of famous structures of antiquity, such as the Parthenon and open theatres, which the detainees were forced to build as a way of demonstrating to them that the ancient Greek 'spirit' was at odds with their so-called Slavo-communism. Upon witnessing such prodigious displays of craftsmanship during a visit to Makronisos in August 1949, Robert Miner (Second Secretary of the U.S. Embassy in Athens) wrote: 'When I remarked on the apparent wealth of artistic talent on Makronisos, Colonel Bairaktaris [the general director of Makronisos] said, only half humorously, that all the young intellectuals in Greece had passed through this camp' (Quoted in Polymeris Voglis, *Becoming a Subject: Political Prisoners during the Greek Civil War*, New York: Berghahn Books, 2002, p. 114, n38).

54. Yannis Papatheodorou, 'The "Densely Populated Wilderness" of the Poets of Makronisos: Exilic Writings', in Stratis Bournazos and Tasos Sakellaropoulos (eds), *Historical Place and Historical Memory: The Example of Makronisos* [Greek] (Athens: Philistor, 2000), p. 238.

to sign 'declarations of repentance' (δηλώσεις μετάνοιας), stating that they no longer had any links with communism. Nearly all would initially refuse, and would then be savagely set upon by the Military Police (Αστυνομία Μονάδας / Αλφαμίτες, ΑΜ), a special unit charged with internal security; this corps became synonymous with torture and included members of extreme right-wing groups but also repentant detainees seeking to provide proof of their own 'rehabilitation'. The beatings were so excruciating that sooner or later nearly everyone relented. As one camp commander warned, 'only the dead don't sign'.[55] But anyone brave enough to refuse signing would be isolated into a small barbedwire cage (σύρμα), made to carry or break stones from sunrise to sunset, given minimal food and water, while being bludgeoned by guards, until the detainee was so crushed in body and spirit that they too finally recanted.[56]

Remarkably, Leivaditis never signed.[57] His fate and that of his fellow detainees was to significantly change after the March 1950 elections, when Nikolaos Plastiras' new Centre Union party won on a platform of reconciliation and, combined with increased domestic and international pressure, put an end to the detention of civilians, thus dissolving OAM. The remaining 'unredeemed' exiles on Makronisos were transferred in mid-1950 to Aghios Eustratios, locally known as Ai Stratis, a small and secluded island in the northern Aegean, about 30 km southwest of Lemnos. Although arid and rocky, Ai Stratis was far more hospitable to the 3,500 arrivals from Makronisos, allowing them greater autonomy and better living conditions. One of these arrivals, Dimitris Photiades (the former editor of *Elefthera Grammata*, who had to hand over the editorship to others upon his arrest in late 1948), recalled: 'When

---

55. Quoted in Rena Levkaditou-Papantoniou, *Makronisos: A Reminder ... About What Happened and What Was Written* [Greek] (Athens: Entos Editions, 2017), p. 59.

56. On this Sisyphean torture of the stone, and other methods of torture which drove many to madness or suicide, see Panourgiá, *Dangerous Citizens*, pp. 92–93, and Levkaditou-Papantoniou, *Makronisos*, pp. 87–108. For a masterful literary depiction of the farcical and dehumanizing nature of these tortures, see Andreas Fragkias' novel *Λοιμός* ('Pestilence', 1972, unfortunately not yet translated into English), where, for example, detainees are ordered to catch at least twenty flies each day, otherwise they will be deprived of water and food; and when a transfer of water is required for building a new structure, the authorities demand that this be done by detainees carrying the water in their own mouths! And if they swallow, they are punished. See also Pantelis Voulgaris' 1976 film, *Happy Day*, which draws upon Fragkias' novel.

57. Neither did Ritsos, who seems to have been protected from punishment by his standing, both nationally and internationally, as a literary figure. (See, for example, the testimony of Manthos Kietsis, as recorded by Tatiana Gritsi-Milliex, in *Diavazo* [Greek], no. 205, 21 December 1988, pp. 47–51.) It is possible that Ritsos was also in a position to place at least some detainees under his protection, and Leivaditis, as a close friend since the early 1940s, may have been one such fortunate person.

we disembarked on Ai Stratis we thought we had gone from hell to heaven. Houses, women, children, a coffee-house and grocery and, the most precious of all, trees and wells with drinkable water.'[58] For Leivaditis, however, these simple freedoms and pleasures would have been more than offset by the news of the death of his much beloved mother, which reached him when still in Makronisos:

> Now you have left, mother, and I didn't get to see you.
> You died as I was devouring the horizon with my eyes
> behind barbedwire
> trying to find where our house might be
> trying to find a small spark from the great fireplace of your affection.[59]

After more than a year on Ai Stratis, Leivaditis is transferred to Athens, but as a detainee still and so he finds himself in Chatzikosta Prison again. Thanks to the intervention of a prison doctor, who declares Leivaditis a consumptive, he is released by the end of 1951. But even then he is released only as an 'αδειούχος εξόριστος': literally, an exiled individual on leave; more precisely, a detainee who has been granted permission to return to the general community, but only conditionally (on the condition, e.g. of reporting to the police or security services on a regular basis), and thus with the risk of arbitrary arrest always hanging over his head.

Politics and Poetry

Leivaditis seriously contemplated suicide on three occasions over the course of his life, the first of these when he was detained on the island prison camps, in despair at reaching 28 years of age without having a single book to his name.[60] However, it was not long before he would begin publishing poetry that was not only far removed from the earlier works discussed above, but that also had the capacity to touch and transform readers in ways that many of contemporaries could not succeed in doing. It could be said that in Makronisos Leivaditis found his voice, a strikingly simple but compelling voice emerging out of his lived experience of love and war, and one that continues to resonate with contemporary audiences.

---

58. Photiades, *Reminiscences*, p. 365.
59. Leivaditis, 'The Man with the Drum', *Poetry*, vol. 1: 1950–1966 [Greek] (Athens: Metronomos, 2015), p. 193.
60. See Lila Kourkoulakou, 'Memories and a Cinematic Portrait', in *I Lexi* [Greek], no. 130, November–December 1995, p. 834.

This singular voice first came to light in an eight-page groundbreaking feature on Makronisos poetry published in a 1950 issue of *Elefthera Grammata*.[61] Four poems were included, which were smuggled out of the camps to become the earliest published poems on Makronisos. Apart from Leivaditis, there were contributions from Ritsos (excerpts from his 38-stanza-long 'Letter to Joliet-Curie', seeking to bring the plight of the detainees to the attention of the West), the highly esteemed theatre and film actor Tsavalas Karousos (who contributed the poem, 'A Night in the Camp', where the night groans as heavily as the inmates) and Kostas Koulouphakos (whose poem, 'On the 6th of May', commemorates a school friend hung by the Germans in 1944).

Leivaditis' contribution, 'Απλή κουβέντα' (Simple Words), rivals that of Ritsos' in power and technique. Direct and impassioned, the poem conveys an ethics and aesthetics of simplicity:

> I would like to speak simply
> the way you unbutton your shirt
> and reveal an old scar
> the way you feel cold at the elbow, and turn
> to find holes in what you're wearing
> the way a prisoner sits down and delouses his singlet.
> To speak of whether I might return someday
> carrying a filthy mess tin brimming with exile
> carrying in my pockets two clenched fists
> to speak simply [...]
>
> It is enough for us to speak simply
> the way one loves
> the way we die
> simply.

As suggested by these lines with which the poem opens and closes, simplicity is not advocated for its own sake but because of its relationship with solidarity, specifically solidarity with comrades and common folk and their struggle for freedom and justice. It's not difficult to identify in the call 'to speak simply' a critique of the poetry of the older, 1930s generation represented by the sophistication of Seferis and the surrealism of Embeirikos and Elytis. Against 'the sun-drinking poet', Elytis, and his pretensions of developing a 'metaphysics of the sun', Leivaditis pulls poetry back down to the earth and stones of the camps, to the wind and cold battering the dirty and diseased bodies of his comrades:

---

61. See *Elefthera Grammata*, vols 2–4, October–December 1950, pp. 123–30.

We once dreamed of becoming great poets
we spoke of the sun
now our heart pierces us like nails in our boots
in the past we'd say: sky, now we say: courage
we're no longer poets but merely
men
with lice, stinking breath and big dreams.

Here we find the beginnings of Leivaditis' political turn, following in the footsteps of the wartime movement of 'resistance poetry', which sought not to replace poetry with ideology but to undermine the traditional distinction between *poiesis* and *praxis*. The aim, in other words, was a 'committed literature', in the Sartrean sense of *littérature engagée*, engaged not with itself (art-for-art's sake) or with ideal forms or abstractions, but with particular historical situations, provoking readers to a greater consciousness of their alienation but also of the possibilities for its transcendence through freedom. Literature, in this view, is in the service of liberation. As Sartre states, 'the writer, a free man addressing free men, has only one subject – freedom'.[62] It's impossible (almost as a matter of definition) for a good novel or poem to promote injustice; it must rather bear witness to the times, showing solidarity with the victims, rebelling against oppression and providing a basis for hope. Despite the criticisms often levelled against such attempts at mixing politics and poetry, the Occupation in Greece had the effect of radicalizing writers around the common cause of national liberation, while the post-war experience of fratricide helped to create a diverse and influential tradition of leftist, often communist, poetry, spearheaded by Leivaditis' longtime mentor, Ritsos.

Leivaditis first set out in this tradition with 'Simple Words', which was later revised and republished in his 1956 collection *The Man with the Drum*, in a section entitled 'Makronisos (1950)'. This part of the book included two more poems: 'Παραμονή Χριστουγέννων' (Christmas Eve) and 'Μη σημαδέψεις την καρδιά μου' (Don't Take Aim At My Heart). The latter has in fact become something of a minor classic, its popularity and originality having much to do with its daring approach to solidarity, this time not between comrades but between enemies: two childhood friends occupying opposite sides of the civil war, with one about to execute the other. The solidarity in this case is also entirely one-directional, even Christ-like, in the sense that the connection is recognized only by one person (the narrator), this further illustrating how violence and ideology have dehumanized and desensitized these former friends.

---

62. Jean-Paul Sartre, *What Is Literature?* trans. Bernard Frechtman (London: Routledge, 2001), p. 48.

So that readers might fully appreciate this short but brilliant poem, a transla-
tion has been appended to the present triptych. In the meantime, the following
account from Tasos Vournas (a prominent leftist writer who was to become a
close friend of Leivaditis' and a keen advocate of his work) may provide some
idea of the impact the poem had upon its earliest readers:

> I remember it was around 1950. The civil war had recently ended. And
> news began to appear in the 'democratic' [i.e. left-wing] press from the
> 'wounded birds' which would break the barriers surrounding Makronisos
> and reveal a nightmare even more horrifying than the most hellish fan-
> tasy. And so one day there arrived a little piece of paper, folded and
> crumpled in a million places, to add to the testimonies continuously
> coming from *over there*. It was a poem. Signed: *Tasos Leivaditis*. Entitled:
> 'Don't take aim at my heart'. We devoured it, more so as to learn about
> the reactions of a poet than from any desire at the time for literary inter-
> course. Bent over the paper, we noticed our faces had become drenched
> in those 'infant tears' spoken of by Homer. The verses were like shots
> fired straight to our heart:

> > Guard, my brother
> > guard, my brother
> > I can hear you walking on the snow
> > I can hear you coughing in the cold
> > I know you, brother
> > and you know me.
> > I bet you have a photo of a girl in your pocket ...[63]

Battle at the Edge of the Night

The year after his release from prison, in 1952, Leivaditis published two
poetry books, the first of which was entitled Μάχη στην άκρη της νύχτας (Battle
at the Edge of the Night), which he had begun on Makronisos and completed
on Ai Stratis.[64] The work consists in a gripping description of a single, seem-
ingly endless, wintry night on a prison camp, the identity of which is explicitly

---

63. Quoted in Leondaritis, *The Journalism and Literature of the Left*, pp. 199–200; Vournas'
    article was originally published in the *Avghe* newspaper on 9 January 1966.
64. Despite what is commonly stated by both scholars and library catalogues, Leivaditis'
    first two poetry books (*Battle at the Edge of the Night* and *This Star Is For All Of Us*) were
    not published by Kedros Publications. Kedros was established in Athens in December
    1954, and only later would it go on to be Leivaditis' publisher.

referenced only in the work's subtitle (*The Chronicle of Makronisos*), which is itself omitted from the Collected Works edition. There is a certain indistinctness therefore to the location and the characters, thus inviting the reader to place the action at just about any of the numerous camps, gulags, or 'rehabilitation centres' of the last century. Although written as a single poem, the work is split into a series of short, episodic scenes (15 in all), frequently shifting in perspective and giving the narrative a film-like feel. In free verse, in language that is simple and lucid but also dense and packed with emotion (Ilinskaya has spoken of the work's 'naturalistic rawness'[65]), Leivaditis gives a dramatic eyewitness account (heightened by the use of the present tense, repetition and dialogue) of the marches, tortures and executions to which the detainees are subjected.

The memorable opening scene is a particularly good demonstration of Leivaditis' technique of mirroring severe physical conditions with crises in subjectivity: in short, sharp lines, a pitch-black, chilly and desolate landscape emerges as the backdrop for the psychological topography of fear, anguish and despair that constitutes the prisoners' consciousness. It is a nightmarish setting, and one that brings about disorientation not only in space but also in time, as the sentries waiting for their replacement grow increasingly anxious about their inability to see in the dark and keep asking, 'what time is it?' The darkness here is not only material and meteorological, but epistemological and existential as well: the standard coordinates collapse, pushing hope for a better world out of reach.

The next scene switches to the prisoners' perspective, as they march under armed guard through rain and mud at night, not knowing where they are being taken. The darkness is likened to 'a black wall', the mud to 'a sure grave', while the prisoners contend with cold and wind, in shabby uniforms and shabbier health ('covered in spots', a wooden leg, facial scars, a missing arm), unable to speak or even think, and walking with 'numb soles'. Yet solidarity is not lost: 'give me your hand' is repeatedly placed at the end of several stanzas, much like a refrain.

In the ensuing scene, a prisoner who has been condemned to death is made to dig his own grave, overseen by six soldiers. As the wind intensifies, he is executed and quickly buried. The repetition of 'bitter' no less than eight times in this scene poignantly marks the injustice and indignity of the execution. In the scenes that follow, another prisoner has kerosene poured on him and is set alight; a young detainee is hung by the hands, interrogated and mercilessly tortured. In the most harrowing scene of all, involving a sudden explosion

---

65. Sonia Ilinskaya, *The Fate of a Generation: A Contribution to the Study of Postwar Political Poetry in Greece* [Greek], 6th ed. (Athens: Kedros, 1986), p. 57.

of gunfire and howls, as 'bullets rivet the darkness' and defenceless prisoners madly scramble, Leivaditis is drawing upon the well-known massacre at Makronisos of 29 February–1 March 1948 when a hunger strike was brutally crushed by the Military Police who opened fire on unarmed detainees, killing around 50–60 and injuring another 200.[66]

As we progress through terrible scenes like these, it becomes clear that we are witnessing a Manichean battle between two fiercely opposed groups, not dissimilar to the two factions of the Greek civil war. On one side, there are the armed and powerful victors who are also the victimizers. On the other side, there are the vanquished victims, passive and oppressed. Interestingly, the victors, despite their position of military strength, are characterized by fear (the commander never dares to leave his room), guilt (the patrol officer kills himself), madness (the bugler sounds his instrument all through the night), and a lack of compassion and moral direction (blindly obeying commands: 'That's the order'). In this highly homogeneous group individuality has disappeared and only ranks and titles remain, and so it's easy for these soldiers to forget 'that tears are the same in everyone / that the world suffices for everyone'. In short, they have lost their conscience and humanity: they are 'faces without faces', no longer able to 'hear their hearts'. The vanquished, by contrast, might be overpowered in a physical sense, but possess moral strength, fortitude and integrity. They too act as a collective (note the frequent use of 'we'), but one guided by a properly functioning moral compass: they act with solidarity and self-sacrifice, refusing to betray their comrades even if that means torture and execution.

The picture, however, is complicated by the suggestion that at least some oppressors are victims themselves, which is why they are presented with a degree of leniency: 'the soldiers lift their collars / not even they know [who or what is to blame]'. Some oppressors, then, may be excused to some extent for their ignorance, while others might be redeemed by acts of goodness, like the soldier who offers his flask of water to the prisoners who were attacked in the massacre. The 'good' (oppressed) side, nonetheless, is never presented with any flaws, at least not any serious ones: they display no evidence of, for example, selfishness, immorality, or cowardly behaviour. What they display, rather, is

---

66. For further details on this massacre, see Voglis, *Becoming a Subject*, pp. 148–51; Geladopoulos, *Makronisos*, pp. 66–68; and Levkaditou-Papantoniou, *Makronisos*, pp. 45–54 (which includes eyewitness accounts). It is difficult to determine the exact number of victims, and here I rely on Raftopoulos' estimate in *Aris Alexandrou*, p. 166. Ritsos speaks of '300 murdered' in his poem, 'A. B. C. – Makronisos' (see Ritsos, *Petrified Time: Poems from Makronisos*, trans. Martin McKinsey and Scott King (Northfield: Red Dragonfly Press, 2014), pp. 93, 97).

a heroic resistance and optimism in the most horrific conditions, as exemplified by the two men held in separate cells in the closing scene. Although badly burnt and beaten ('Their legs broken / their arms twisted'), they are not diminished or defeated. Instead, they heap scorn on their executioners (their 'laughter humiliated the enemy') and retain their faith in justice and eventual victory. The poem ends by repeating their own words, words Leivaditis himself would have often uttered and heard in Makronisos: *The sun is for all people. The day is near. We will go on.*

This Star Is For All Of Us

Published soon after *Battle, Αυτό το αστέρι είναι για όλους μας* (This Star Is For All Of Us) continues the preoccupation with the civil war and island camps, but with far greater emphasis on the interior life, particularly that of the narrator in relationship to his beloved. Leivaditis dedicated the book to his wife, Maria, and the poem reads like a love letter to her (though an unsent one, as there is no indication of a response). Against the stereotype of the communist as dour ideologue, Leivaditis finely fuses political commitment with a romantic sensibility, in the tradition of Aragon's poems about 'Elsa's Eyes' (inspired by his wife, Elsa Triolet) and Neruda's sonnets to his (third) wife, Matilde Urrutia. In *Star*, however, *eros* always stands in tension with *polemos*: the narrator's tender and affectionate address to his beloved has the effect of marking a sharp contrast between the violent, death-ridden reality outside and the lovers' subjective experience of life-affirming, loving devotion.

Star, compared with *Battle*, has fewer sections but lengthier lines; the language remains simple and direct, but is more descriptive and expressive, reaching great lyrical and sensual heights, infused with a profound tenderness, when the narrator addresses or speaks of his beloved. The poem's structure is also more intricate. Although the poem opens with the civil war – National Army soldiers are leaving for the battlefield, the White Terror campaign is in full swing – the narrative does not take a linear progression but is interrupted by past events and by the future as it breaks in upon the present. Commentators have rightly read the work as embodying a marxist-style dialectical progression that begins (in Part III) with a whimsical account of the narrator as a child, waiting, longing and even making preparations for the arrival of his beloved.[67] The narrator eventually moves beyond his ego-centric predicament of sadness and emptiness when he encounters his beloved, instantly recognizing her

---

67. See Benatsis, *Tasos Leivaditis' Poetic Mythology*, pp. 102–14; and Eratosthenis Kapsomenos, *'This Star Is For All Of Us*: Natural and Social Values in Leivaditis', *Diavazo* [Greek], no. 228, 13 December 1989, pp. 26–32.

when they first meet: 'Because before you came into my life / you had long
lived in my dreams.' They quickly fall in love and move in together, enjoying
a domestic life abounding with homely pleasures and scents, and soon start a
family. 'How lovely it was to be alive!' the narrator recalls, reflecting his tran-
sition to an other-centric state of fulfillment and happiness.

But this could not last. The call of conscience, specifically 'the eyes of my
neighbour whose four children were killed', compels the narrator to make the
painful decision to leave the bliss of home life and his pregnant wife behind
and to join his comrades in battle: 'We had to go our separate ways, Maria,
/ to separate so that people separate no more.' Before he could do so, how-
ever, his house was raided, and he was arrested and detained in a prison camp
(Parts I and III). And so, he returns once again to a condition of deprivation,
this time one of imprisonment and subjugation.

At the beginning of Part II, we thus find the narrator in a bleak and ter-
rifying prison camp like that of Makronisos, and feeling as though 'the last
memory upon the earth had died'. Amidst the torture of the stone, rifle butt
blows, scanty food, amputated arms and increasing deaths and executions
('The empty mess tins quickly multiply in the corner'), the narrator achieves
a deeper level of consciousness. His experience of solidarity with the other
detainees enables him to rise to a newfound awareness, from the private 'we'
of his relationship with his beloved to the universal 'we' embracing all people,
especially those ill-treated and exploited. Paradoxically, it is this movement
towards the collective that allows him to rediscover his beloved:

> I shared the bread with my neighbour as though I were sharing it
>   with you
> and as I reached out to grasp someone's hand, I found your hand
> and as I stooped to listen to some voice, I found your voice.

> Those who separated us are the same ones now returning you to me.

Separation is overcome via solidarity, and the dichotomy between the indi-
vidual and the communal is (to use Hegel's term) 'sublated', transcended by
being elevated to a higher plane where the previous condition of fulfillment is
restored but now in a transfigured state.

From this vantage point, the narrator (in Part IV) turns his mind to his
beloved without self-indulgent sentimentality, but with conviction in the
justice and future triumph of their cause, with the confidence that they will
be reunited and live on (in the generations to come) even if he ends up killed
and she remarries. The poem ends (in Part V) with a rapturous foretaste of
this future utopia, which intrudes into the present in the manner of a 'realized

eschatology' with the coming of spring, sunshine and song, with a spirit of optimism amongst farmers and workers busily constructing a better world, and a sense of brotherhood between all people: an old woman in faraway Asia is knitting socks that will be worn someday by the narrator's daughter. The love between the narrator and his beloved is now *universalized:* it is recognized as a vindication of, but also a point of identification with, all those who have been murdered or marginalized. It is an all-encompassing (one could call it 'pantheistic') love, integrating everything and everyone, living and dead, thus defeating despair and oblivion. That's why Leivaditis chose for his title not '*a* star', one that only a select few (e.g. astronomers) can make out, but '*this* star', a celestial object bright enough to be perceived *by everyone* and providing illumination to all in dark times. Such stars are the eternal values of love, peace, justice and solidarity.[68]

The Wind at the Crossroads of the World

Star was hailed as 'one of the best poems to see the light of day in recent years',[69] while Markos Avgheris, a stalwart of the literary Left, similarly described the book as 'distinguishing itself from recent poetry with a new and powerful light'.[70] With Leivaditis' next work, Φυσάει στα σταυροδρόμια του κόσμου (The Wind at the Crossroads of the World), published in 1953, the praise intensified and broadened to the international level, but at home Leivaditis would once more be persecuted and imprisoned.

The work is set in the early Cold War era, as Greece passes from one violent conflict to another, this time funded by the Americans and their anti-communist crusade. In the frigid cold, the compromised Greek collaborators are leading a requiem for the fallen in World War II, against the background of a city (that is not named but could well be Athens) reduced to misery and wretchedness: slums, orphanages, brothels, child asylums, soup kitchens. A dualism, parallel to that in *Battle*, is thereby created between the rulers and the masses: the degenerate bourgeoisie, with their power, status and beauty, ruling over the proletarians who are portrayed sympathetically despite (or because of) their abject condition. Unlike *Battle*, however, the exploited workers and the destitute unemployed are not as passive and powerless as they are in

---

68. Interestingly, in September 2020, Leivaditis' star symbolism was appropriated by the main opposition party Syriza in its rebranding campaign. In a promotional video to introduce the campaign, party leader, Alexis Tsipras, mentions Leivaditis and quotes the title of his book against the background of the party's new logo which features a star.
69. Anonymous review published in the *Avghe* newspaper, 8 December 1952.
70. Markos Avgheris, 'The Poetry of Tasos Leivaditis', [Greek] *Avghe* newspaper, 13 October 1953.

the earlier work: now hardened and enraged (note the descriptions of their facial features), they are on the verge of a revolution (prepared in secret: 'Two workers converse in hushed tones'), about to push back after having been pushed to the edge for so long: 'A coal worker's eyes against his blackened face / like red emergency lights in the night.'

Speeches are given by a minister and a general, calling people to arms and to defend the fatherland. But the crowd, weary and hungry, pays little attention to these bombastic orations, which are in any case drowned out by the roaring wind. When the wind abates and there is complete silence, the narrative suddenly shifts to an apocalyptic plane. The sky turns red, as does the ground, 'like blood'. The war dead – the resistance fighters who were being cynically celebrated by the collaborators – emerge from the horizon and from under the earth. These zombie-like figures slowly advance in long files, in the thousands, staggering towards all corners of the earth, in the midst of cannonfire and smoke. 'And the horizons were lit up red as though the earth was on fire.' It makes for a terrifying sight: mutilated, disembowelled and disfigured soldiers, just as they were at the moment of death. The war-mongering elites are crushed, and in an arresting image of just deserts, 'The top hats tumble / the furs turn back into animals and bite them at the neck'. Workers come together from all parts of the world, over-coming what previously divided them (religion, nationalism) and join the war dead, marching in 'a forest of raised fists' and calling for justice and peace. The wind starts up again, a new day dawns, 'and with their hard, callused hands' the people begin 'laying out on the red horizon / the broad gestures of a new destiny'.

As indicated by this narrative outline, one of the distinguishing features of the work is the unexpected turn towards the end from realism to sur-realism – a ghoulish and grotesque surrealism, not unlike Francis Bacon's paintings of fleshy, contorted, howling, animalistic figures (many of these paintings responding, like Leivaditis' poem, to the savagery of World War II). If the imagery is reminiscent of Bacon, the language often recalls the biblical and liturgical traditions of the Orthodox Church, perhaps in imita-tion of (as many have claimed) Aleksandr Blok's famous poem, 'The Twelve' (1918), which also has a tempestuous wind coursing through it and enigmatic-ally ends with twelve Red Guards being led by Christ.[71] Leivaditis' poem, like

---

71. Note in particular how Blok's poem begins much like Leivaditis' *Wind*:
    Black night,
    White snow.
    Wind O wind!
    It knocks you down as you go.
    Wind O wind –Through God's world blowing. (Jack Lindsay trans.)

Blok's, has the form of a divine epiphany, a second coming, as the war dead
are resurrected to bring down the judgement of God ('ready to strike'), in the
style of the Old Testament prophets. As this shows, Leivaditis' work, from the
very beginning, has never been purely realistic or naturalistic, but is frequently
interpenetrated by the magical and metaphysical, the apocalyptic and mys-
tical.[72] Yet Leivaditis makes it clear that the world the people are fighting to
build will have no place for religion: God is dethroned, the church discredited
and theology replaced by humanistic ideals.

One of the ways in which religion is discredited in this work is through
biting satire. The reality of beggars starving on the streets is juxtaposed with
contented priests spouting obscene theodicies, justifying the status quo. The
political class too is made to look stupid and ridiculous, while the requiem and
the accompanying rally play out like a tragic comedy: 'Heil Hitler! / oh! my
apologies / I meant to say: The Freedom of the Fatherland.' To cut through
their lies the narrative lens moves swiftly, as though carried by the wind,
from one poor and desperate person to another, taking in bits of dialogue, or
making quick but precise (snapshot-like) observations. The narrative, model-
ling the rush and fury of the wind, becomes brisk and rapid in tempo and loud
and rowdy in volume, but also highly lyrical – which may explain why *Wind*
has been successfully set to music by many.[73]

The Red Scare in Greece

With the publication of *Wind*, Leivaditis finally arrived as an important new
voice in modern Greek literature. The critics were unanimous. Avgheris wrote:

> When reading Leivaditis' new work, *The Wind at the Crossroads of the
> World*, we are transported every so often from astonishment to wonder
> [...] Nothing in it is calculated or preconceived, nothing is affected or
> counterfeit, everything bears the stamp of truth, authenticity and inspir-
> ation, pulsing with genuine passion.

See also John Garrard, '*The Twelve:* Blok's Apocalypse', *Religion & Literature*
(2003), pp. 45–72, which shows how Blok's poem creatively reworks the Book of
Revelation.

72. For a defence of this reading, see Mihalis G. Meraklis, 'A Contribution to the
Restoration of a Broken Unity', in *I Lexi* [Greek], no. 130, November–December
1995, pp. 746–55; and Xeni Skartsis, 'The Religious Dimension in Leivaditis' Poetry',
Themata Logotechnias [Greek], no. 56, 2017, pp. 141–55.

73. Including the prominent composer Yiorgos Tsagkaris, and the ensemble 'Onar', led by
the singer Penny Ramantani.

In concluding his review, Avgheris compares *Wind* with *Star*, and states:

> *Wind* is stylistically tighter, textually more pregnant with meaning and
> vivid juxtapositions, richer in imagery, the execution firmer, and in
> comparison with the preceding work stands one step higher: the poet
> is moving up, it's obvious that he is in a felicitous place, he's on fire, in
> a state of sheer euphoria and strength. He promises many and great
> things.[74]

Even the influential critic and Seferis scholar, Andreas Karantonis, who
cannot be charged with any bias in favour of leftist literature, was enthusiastic
about *Wind*:

> Like a sudden squall overturning the tables of seaside restaurants,
> carrying off roofs and tearing out trees, Leivaditis seizes words, a multi-
> tude of words and images, wild and dark images and pieces them
> together, endlessly, so as to convey his impressive vision – which, in the
> final analysis, is an aggregation of unfastened 'objects and values' that
> the catastrophic, revolutionary wind raises up high in a swirl. This is
> a poem which resists analysis and evaluation. You either feel it or you
> don't.[75]

State authorities, numbed by power and ideology, definitely didn't 'feel
it'. *Wind* was published in September 1953, and on 9 December the book
was banned by the public prosecutor for violating Law 509 and police were
ordered to confiscate all copies from bookstores and publishing houses. The
next day (10 December), the newspaper *Avghe* (Dawn) reported that a 'painful
impression' had been made not only in literary circles but also in the wider
community, which had come to love and applaud the book. 'The seizure of
the book yesterday', the newspaper stated, 'is being viewed as an attempt at
muzzling progressive thinkers and as a typical manifestation of McCarthyism
in our country'.[76]

After a seven-month silence about his fate, Leivaditis was formally charged
in the middle of 1954 with 'high treason' and 'sedition'; and in December was

---

74. Avgheris, 'The Poetry of Tasos Leivaditis', [Greek] *Avghe* newspaper, October 13, 1953.
    Similar high praise of *Wind* was given by Tasos Vournas in his review of *The Man with
    the Drum*, published in *Avghe* on 8 July 1956.
75. Andreas Karantonis, *Our Poetry After Seferis* [Greek] (Athens: Dodonis, 1976), p. 224.
76. 'Police Seize Poetry Book', *Avghe* [Greek], 10 December 1953.

sent back to prison, while awaiting trial.[77] But he refused to be silenced. From behind bars, he wrote letters of protest to the press, and published in *Avghe* an excerpt from his poem, 'The Man with the Drum', where a poet who has been blacklisted responds by taking to the streets and raucously playing the drums

> to keep people awake
> to keep life awake
> to shout in the night
> that however much they kill us
> we
> exist
> louder still
> making the entire land
> tremble and quiver in the night![78]

Leivaditis also appealed to overseas writers and organizations, including the World Federation of Democratic Youth,[79] and a powerful support movement, both domestic and worldwide, soon arose.

Although it might seem strange today that a poetry book espousing the cause of peace would be banned and its author arrested, this was not at all unusual at the time. This was the height of the Cold War, a highly polarized political climate, with repression, show trials, purges and executions on both sides of the Iron Curtain. While, for example, Stalin was orchestrating the Doctors' Plot in 1953, imprisoning (mainly Jewish) doctors for alleged conspiracy, the House Un-American Activities Committee (HUAC) was conducting investigations into communist infiltration into American society, and in particular the film industry, calling eleven Hollywood figures to testify

---

77. On this occasion, Leivaditis was detained in Vourla Prison (Φυλακές Βούρλων), located in the Drapetsona suburb of Piraeus. The prisons of Greece in 1954, Vourla included, were flooded with arrested communists. On 17 July 1955, a daring escape from Vourla took place, with 27 communists fleeing, causing a sensation in the press and great embarrassment to the government. It's quite possible that Leivaditis knew about the escape, which was being meticulously planned and prepared while he was imprisoned.

78. Published in *Avghe* on 10 December 1954. This was to become, in amended form, the beginning and end of the poem as it appeared in Leivaditis' 1956 collection, *The Man with the Drum*.

79. The World Federation of Democratic Youth (WFDY) was founded in London in 1945 as a global non-governmental organization promoting peace and human rights, but tended to be employed during the Cold War as a platform for communist ideology. Leivaditis' letter to WFDY is published in Yiorgos Theocharis, 'The Persecution of Leivaditis', *To Dendro* [Greek], no. 171–72, February 2009, pp. 39–41.

in 1947, but only one, the visiting German dramatist Bertolt Brecht, choosing to answer questions (and giving a legendary performance during a three-hour interrogation). The work of the HUAC paved the way for the militant campaign waged by Senator Joseph McCarthy in the early 1950s, and this anticommunist hysteria or 'Red Scare' was to be exported to Greece.[80]

The steps taken in post-war Greece towards economic reconstruction would be undermined by the lack of reconciliation between the hostile parties. As Greece entered in 1952 an 11-year period of uninterrupted right-wing rule, the ideological divisions deepened, transforming the country into what has been called an 'apartheid' state separating 'national-minded' citizens from those stigmatized as communists, fellow-travellers or sympathizers.[81] During this shift towards the authoritarian right, the wartime emergency laws remained in effect and continued to be used to persecute leftists and outlaw the KKE (which moved its headquarters to Bucharest and was replaced domestically by the more broadly leftist United Democratic Left, EDA). And those, like Leivaditis, who were released from the camps were treated with utmost suspicion, were subjected to surveillance and harassment, if not worse, and were denied 'certificates of loyalty' and all the social benefits these made possible (e.g. state employment, university entrance, driver's license, passport). In this repressive atmosphere, even to be seen holding the leftist (EDA-sponsored) *Avghe* newspaper (which began circulating in 1952 and employed Leivaditis as a literary critic from 1954) could land one in trouble with the police. Trials of leftists, often on fabricated charges and leading to death sentences, became commonplace, as demonstrated by the sensational trials of Nikos Nikiforidis (executed on 5 March 1951, at 23 years of age, for participating in the communist-led peace movement), Nikos Beloyannis, 'the man with the carnation' (charged with espionage and executed on 30 March 1952, arousing a storm of protest in Greece and abroad) and Nikos Ploumpidis (executed on 14 August 1954 for his role in the underground communist network).

The Trial

In these circumstances, it's no great surprise that Leivaditis too would be put on trial, especially given *Wind*'s mocking censure of Greece's leaders and

---

80. See Minas Samatas, 'Greek McCarthyism: A Comparative Assessment of Greek Post-Civil War Repressive Anticommunism and the U.S. Truman–McCarthy Era', *Journal of the Hellenic Diaspora*, vol. 13, 1986, pp. 5–75.

81. See Constantine Tsoucalas, 'The Ideological Impact of the Civil War', in John O. Iatrides (ed.), *Greece in the 1940s: A Nation in Crisis* (Hanover: University Press of New England, 1981), p. 328.

their imperialist and capitalist patrons, and the book's depiction towards the end of violent retribution.[82] The five-member Court of Appeal convened on 10 February 1955, to hear the case against Leivaditis and, at the same time, against Andreas Pagkalos for his translation of Stalin's *Economic Problems of Socialism in the USSR.*

The trial, before a packed courtroom, began with the testimony of witnesses against the accused. These witnesses predictably included two police officers, one of whom, Ioannis Karahalios, went on to an 'illustrious' career as head of security services and in a later trial, in November 1975, acted as a defence witness for some of the most vicious torturers in the security services of the 1967–74 dictatorial regime. More surprising, however, was the appearance on the witness stand of the president of the Athens Bar Association, Athanasios Zervopoulos, who conceded that he had only read parts of Leivaditis' book; and of the distinguished academic, Yiorgos Sakellariou (1888–1964). The latter was a professor at the University of Athens who had studied widely in philosophy and psychology, both in Europe and the United States, including Princeton and Columbia universities. Leivaditis' book, the professor stated, should be judged as an 'αλογοτέχνημα' (a literary work bereft of rationality, '*logos*') which 'seeks to denigrate the values and way of life of contemporary Greek society'. The way in which the book was written is 'demonic, and is evidence also of the author's irrationality, for whoever rejects the foundational principles of our nation could not be of sound mind'.[83] This was the testimony of someone who is regarded as pioneering the study of psychology in higher education in Greece.

The witnesses in defence of the accused were then called, and their testimony in conjunction with Leivaditis' own 'apologia' and his lawyer's closing argument not only unmasked the flimsy and preposterous nature of the charges, but also exhibited the depth of Leivaditis' commitment to the highest artistic and humanistic ideals.[84] It did not take long for the judges to reach their verdict: both Leivaditis and Pagkalos were acquitted, and their seized books subsequently restored. The verdict was interpreted by many on the Left

---

82. Interestingly, the original edition of *Wind* included several passages which were later excised. One of these, which is likely to have provoked the censors, reads: 'Death dons the mask of a general and travels the world / Adenauer washes his dirty hands with soap made in Buchenwald', referring to the first chancellor of the Federal Republic of Germany, Konrad Adenauer, who ardently opposed communism.

83. Quoted in 'Freedom of Expression On Trial', *Avghe*, 10 February 1955. On the 'betrayal of the intellectuals' (to use Julien Benda's title) in post-war Greece, see Tsoucalas, 'The Ideological Impact of the Civil War', pp. 331–38.

84. For a summary of the court proceedings and the arguments of the defence, see the translated article, 'Literature On Trial', placed in Appendix II.

as a watershed moment, possibly inaugurating a new era in Greek society.
Markos Avgheris commented:

> A castle of darkness and death has shut out life in Greece, and perhaps this
> verdict will be the first breach. Will the pure divinities of freedom, peace
> and humanity begin to breath again? Let's hope so.[85]

From Victory to Defeat

That summer, after his court triumph, Leivaditis was awarded the first prize
in the poetry competition of the fifth World Festival of Youth and Students,
an event organized in part by the World Federation of Democratic Youth, to
whom Leivaditis had earlier appealed. The event was hosted by Warsaw, Poland,
attracting some 26,600 young participants, representing 116 countries. The
festival, first convened in 1947, had morphed by this stage into a propaganda
tool for Soviet communism. For the locals, however, the festival was a chance to
become acquainted with the novel ideas and experiences of youth arriving from
cultures and countries inaccessible to them. Ironically, it was events like this that
would help bring about the Polish Thaw the following year, in 1956, as Poles
began to rise up against Soviet hegemony.

Leivaditis himself was undergoing around this time his own 'thaw'. As
attested by those you knew him well, his commitment to communism up to the
mid-'50s was of an idealistic and uncritical sort.[86] Signs of this can be found
in the triptych, as indicated by its 'us–them' dualism, with its wholly positive
portrayal of the proletarians. More explicitly and embarrassingly, in a poem
published in the wake of Stalin's death on 5 March 1953, Leivaditis described
the Soviet dictator in quasi-religious terms: 'Stalin lives. / Because Stalin is not
a human being who is able to die. / Stalin is hope and bread, he is steel and
Peace.'[87] In a similar vein, Leivaditis published later that year a poem entitled

---

85. Avgheris, 'An Acquittal', *Avghe*, 13 February 1955.
86. See, e.g. Alexandros Argyriou, 'Leivaditis' Poetic Performances: Forty Uninterrupted
    Years', in *I Lexi* [Greek], no. 130, November–December 1995, pp. 721–35.
87. The poem, entitled 'Stalin', was published in *Avghe* on 8 March 1953. Leivaditis insisted
    that his Stalin poem be published in *Epitheorisi Technis*, a leftist literary journal, but
    a broad-based, non-conformist one, promoting a form of Marxism that encouraged
    independence of thought, critical dialogue and self-renewal, and seeking to push leftist
    thought in Greece in new directions and to overcome its then overly dogmatic and con-
    servative forms. Although a founding member of the journal in 1954, and a member
    of its editorial committee, Leivaditis was out of step with colleagues such as Titos
    Patrikios, Kostas Koulouphakos and Dimitris Raftopoulos, who wished to distance the
    journal from orthodox communist circles and so refused to publish Leivaditis' poem.

'Russia', in celebration of the 36th anniversary of the founding of the Soviet Union. In this poem he places Russia in the vanguard of history, in contrast to the doomed world of Western Europe, immobilized by its ossified traditions and capitalist ways. The nadir of the poem is reached upon reference to the 'miracle' of Russia's rapid transformation from a feudal economy to an industrial power: 'Dostoevsky would have wept before this miracle / he would have burnt all his sick books / and would have written his masterpiece by working at the Kuybyshev dam.'[88]

The turning point for Leivaditis came with Khrushchev's secret speech of 25 February 1956, with its denunciation of Stalin's crimes and personality cult, and its initiation of a program of liberalization that sought to break with the oppressive Stalinist past. Khrushchev's revelations caught Leivaditis completely unawares, precipitating a breakdown and driving him again to thoughts of suicide. The defeat of the civil war was bad enough, but being duped by self-made ideological blinkers seemed inexcusable. As he began to move away from the communist cause, his poetry took on a melancholic, resigned, solitary and skeptical tone, but never one that was defeatist, despite his later association with the 'poetry of defeat'. Even in his darkest moments, waking up in the middle of the night from the screams and gunshots of the past, he could recall the love and solidarity of the comrades he suffered alongside with in the hard times of persecution and imprisonment. For, as he writes in *Star*, they were the ones who

when we were cold they cloaked us with their eyes
when we were hungry they apportioned us their heart.
And when we were about to die they spoke to us of life.

Then we too were able to die.

Partly due to this disagreement, Leivaditis departed from the editorial committee, but continued to write for the journal. See Koulouphakos, '*Epitheorisi Technis* and the Presence of the Left in the Cultural Arena', manuscript dated April 1964; first published in *Archeiotaxio* [Greek], no. 2, June 2000, pp. 46–85 (see pp. 54–55).

88. The poem was published in *Avghe* on 8 November 1953. *Kuybyshev:* present-day Samara, in western Russia; at the time it was a closed city and an important industrial and defence hub. During World War II, Stalin built a bunker underneath the city, which he never used.

BATTLE AT THE EDGE OF THE NIGHT

(THE CHRONICLE OF MAKRONISOS)

Brother, are you here?
I can't see you in the dark
and that Corporal of the Guard
is late
what time is it?
I'm cold.

I'm cold too
light a match
what time is it?
how are we going to believe in the world again?
what time is it?

The gate bolted
the road deserted
outposts in the dark
like discarded bones

and that Corporal of the Guard
my God!
he's late
why is the wind blowing?

What time is it in the dark?
What time is it in the rain?
What time is it tonight on all the earth?
What time is it?

*

We move on
our feet are lost in the mud

and can't be heard
one man thirsts
another has no cap
one man's breath stinks
another is covered in spots.
You want to think
but you sink
you want to say something
but your tongue is a slice of mud
your heart a slice of mud
may whoever survive attest to this
the world tonight was mud
give me your hand.

Machine guns under armpits
the soldiers' raincoats
grate
and the rain starts
one man is cold
another carries a sack
one man remembers the sun
another has a wooden leg.
In the past they would walk
and their shoes grate
on the leaves
think about it
on the leaves.

Every so often we step aside
to let the trucks pass
the smell of bread
from a truck transporting army bread
one loaf next to the other
and therefore none cold
give me your hand.

If only
you could stop for a little
to take off your boots
and hurl them
to the heavens
in order to breathe upon

your numb soles
the night is a wall
a black wall
the mud a sure grave
give me your hand.

We move on
one man looks into the distance
another can't see anything
one man has a scar on his face
another halts
and isn't going anywhere
a soldier wanders off
and takes a piss.

If only you could stop
to remove your cap
and hide your face
and bend down to find
find what?
the guard is coughing beside you
you'd like to bite
the half of his ear
above his lifted collar
he crumples his face
and rubs his frozen ear
one man remembers
another spits
one man knew some tales
another has only one hand
give me your hand.
At one moment our steps
pound on the bridge
we sink again in the mud
where are we going?

Give me your hand.

*

The lamp
placed on the ground
a commonplace lamp

six soldiers with weapons
one man digging
bitter night
bitter like injustice.

The mattock goes up and down
sleep still lies on his face
like a bite mark
the frost steals his hands
the earth is speechless at night
we don't have time.

If you asked him what is to blame
he wouldn't know how to answer
may his trespasses be upon us
we all love life
the soldiers lift their collars
not even they know.

And yet tonight before he dies he must
dig his own grave
a hole
in the hard frozen earth.
'That's the order.'

All people in the world are alike
on the road they pay no attention to us
perhaps you've already met him
his head shaven
a frayed jacket
the sky tonight is blind.

Every lump of earth
is a moment lost
every blow a step forward
tomorrow we won't remember anything
bitter night
bitter like oblivion.

If only they'd let him
he would dig up the entire earth
if by digging he could survive

each moment his hands collapse
the lamp grants him a long shadow
and a whitewashed complexion.

If only they'd give him
a small spot to himself
a small spot in a corner somewhere
with room for no more than two feet
albeit naked feet.

If only they'd let him
tell us Corporal sir
are Saturday nights on earth
always beautiful?
are the streets always filled
with children and harmonicas?
Whenever she laughed her eyes would shrink
Corporal sir, she was startled
by the popping sounds of sodas
the world was round
like a small scoured zinc table.

If only they'd let him
merely for a moment
lean on his mattock
and reminisce
you'd better hurry tonight, comrade
bitter night
bitter like indignity.

If only they'd let him
but why have we made
life so short?
why should every blow
be a step forward?
it's cold there, comrades
if only mother would at least tell the truth
and we could find down there
a bit of life.

Meantime the wind gained strength
he didn't cross himself

they quickly covered him
what does the name of a dead man matter?
he had to die
and he died
life will not forget him.

But those six lads
why did they consent to shoot?
may no one find out what happened tonight
bitter night
bitter like submission.

*

A dog somewhere
two statues in the square
the rain playing drums
on the tents.

The roads of the camp
built in accord with town planning rules
– as though it were difficult to die
on poorly constructed roads.

A furrow of water.
It fails to reflect anything.
At an outpost they're playing dice
we have no luck tonight
let's move on.

The lights are on at Headquarters
the Commander stands by the window
his mouth a sharp line.
Pause.

The guard by the door is cold
hey, mate, upstairs it's warm.

Three drunken soldiers
what are they singing?
the bridge is made of timber.

The Commander
terrifies the darkness
he never comes out of his room at night.
Once he shat in his helmet.
A further pause.
Nothing.

*

What's that shining in the dark?
Is it the sun perhaps?

A man is on fire
a man illumines the night
upright in an outpost he illumines the night
they poured kerosene on him
and lit him up
in the world too
a great fire has lit up
let's go and warm up tonight
and see some sky
see whether we are dead
and those two lads
those two soldiers frozen stiff
may they see the time
may they see that it's the time
that no clock
ever showed
when no Corporal of the Guard
even exists
may they see that it's the time
the deepest time of the night
when we become human again.

*

Sitting on the ground
think about it
on the ground
by a ravine suspended
sideways in the night
because it's night, comrade
it's freezing, comrade.

We wait
like spit stuck
to the ground
with nails sunk
into the ground
faces blank
hands blind
one man is drowsy
another chews his collar
one man has lice
another believes in God.

Sitting on the ground
we wait
one man trembles
another has his head bandaged
one man was an umbrella vendor
another is afraid of the night
because it's night, comrade
it's freezing, comrade.

The guards come and go.
Under the torchlight
their teeth must be yellow
no doubt
yellow.
The beam of the torch
reveals a face
unearths a hand
stumbles
upon buckled knees
one man searches his pockets
another searches for sky
one man has regrets
another still has hope.

If only one could
stand up
remember their feet
and stand up
even if only to walk

in the mud
even if only to walk
in the rain
just to stand up
think about it
to stand up
even if he were to get lost
in the dark
because it's night, comrade
it's freezing, comrade.

In order to live
we must deny
that it is night
we must deny
that dawn will arrive.

But since it is night
and since dawn will arrive
we wait
one man predicts what will happen
another completely agrees
one man looks pale
another bites a key.
Someone points with his crutch
but points to something far away.

Sitting on the ground
we wait on the ground
we wait in the night
because it's night, comrade
it's freezing, comrade.

*

Five forage caps in a circle
a nameless captain
a naked youth
hung by the hands
his body furrowed
lacerated by the lashes
his toenails barely touching the floor

the way one springs up to see
a girl laughing behind the bushes.

The captain questions him.

The lash burns the flesh
the pain becomes one with the body
the pain becomes the body itself
then he remembers
a half-built house on the corner
the lad on the scaffolding is hoisting up stone slabs
but why such a young lad
for such large slabs?
his tiny legs suddenly buckled
he lost his grip
the young skull on the paving stone
crushed open
a woman in shock
screaming uninterruptedly: No!

Now he must speak
to survive
he must stop remembering
and start living.
He wants to live
just as you do.

On the table some papers
a one-eyed kepi
his blood on the floor
paints incredible patterns.

The lash creates a furrow
a hand in the dark
the ceiling leaks water
his sister
next to the extinguished brazier
doesn't speak
but looks into the distance.
That night she seemed strange
she talked for hours

he remembers one word only
an incomprehensible word
– joy.
That same night she took off with someone.
We found out she died in childbirth.

Now he must speak
to survive
he must stop dreaming
and start living.
Day lies in the distance still
and he's afraid of breaking
just as you are.

A square of night
upon the open window
his face bloodied
like the carnival masks
which frightened us as children.

The captain lights a cigarette.
The fuse has been lit
his comrade's hands are nimble
any moment it will reach the dynamite
any moment it will be spring.
On the way back they were quiet
every so often their hands would touch
his comrade spoke with a stammer
he was embarrassed and spoke little.

The captain questions him
questions him again
the woman in shock
always screaming:
No!

Now he must speak
to survive
he must stop loving
and start living.
The captain says: Speak!

The lash says: Speak!
The night says to him: Speak!
But the night is short
the comrades many
and he cut out his tongue with his teeth
just as you would have.

*

Don't sleep tonight, comrade
who knows if we'll see each other again
take this matchstick
to keep your eyelids open.
Tomorrow our flags will be flying
if you don't fall asleep.
They'll be blood red
if we stay awake tonight.
Try to think on this:
blood red.
Or take off your boots
and whet your teeth on the hobnails
drowsiness is overcome that way.
The night is long
take care you don't fall asleep.

Holy hatred
give me your hand.

*

Two trucks stopped
their headlights on us.
We
are forever waiting.
The light
like lime powder in our eyes
the night
a sack of bones on our back.

A short, fat captain
wrests himself from the dark
his kepi crooked
a cigarette butt between his teeth

the guards
dip their helmets
and spread out.
Why do they dip them?

A whistle blows
and suddenly
machine guns are heard
rat-a-tat
a scream
a howling sound
machine guns don't listen
rat-a-tat
rat-tat
we run in the dark
where are we going?
on every hilltop they await us
rat-a-tat.

Bullets whistle for a moment
a torn face
bullets rivet the darkness
someone holds up their coat
to hide behind it
no one wants to die
someone else is huddled up
like a small ball of thread
to save himself.

A piece of lead:
do you know what it means
when you're freezing?
When you don't want to die:
do you know
what life means?

Someone is glued to the ground
he would've liked to be
one with the ground.
Machine guns
aren't aware that each of us has a mother

rat-a-tat
rat-tat.
One man tries to make a run for it
another pounces on him
and doesn't let him
a man howls
his entire face a mouth
rat-a-tat.

Bullets bite for a moment
then nothing
bullets can't see in the dark
do you know what life means?
rat-a-tat
rat-tat.

*

Faces with helmets
faces of ash
faces without sky
faces without faces
stomp their boots
so they don't hear their hearts
tighten their belts
so they don't fall in a heap
they are told about the fatherland
but that doesn't warm them up
they were given machine guns
so they would be afraid to die.

They are afraid of the sun, windows,
their eyes, hope.
Our mother used to put us to sleep
with a soft song
what did you do with that song?
At night they hide their hands
so they can sleep
and sleep is for them a scaffold
from which dreams are hurled down.

Night
machine guns are blind

thousands of people are dying
at the moment when the troops
are looking at their barren genitals
and the outposts smell
of semen and hashish.

Others are hiding behind them
those who hide in the dark
made you forget
that tears are the same in everyone
that the world suffices for everyone.
We are talking about you
executioners of the sun
enemies of bread
nothing will save you
one day our boots
will crush your bones.

Night
on your roads people
are unrecognizable
on your roads people
held out their hands.
Who will be able to forget you
night?

But you
you who can still
gaze at the sky
you who tremble
when you shoot
look –
here is our hand.

The world is made for happiness.
Goodbye.

*

This night is bitter
how will we pass
this whole night?

Let me wrap in my coat
this baby.

It's a strange baby
a bit ugly
but still warm
you would've called him
a severed leg
let me cradle him to sleep myself.
Severed from the knee
his knee crushed to a pulp
it's nothing
they cut it with a pickaxe
and it became a bit mashed
nothing more
just a bit more quiet
tell them not to shout
because he's sleepy
tell them not to die
because he's cold.

That leg is a child
your child, my brother
my child
out of four children
you must bury all four
the last one without shoes
wrapped in a hole-riddled shawl
let it sleep next to its mother
you think to yourself
let it sleep.

Whichever road you take
you will meet that child
wherever you hide
that leg is your own
tell them, please, not to shout
because so many people shout
you ask for my name
I no longer remember my name
a piece of paper, they say

and you may live
but how will they live:
thousands of children without bread?
thousands of children without dreams?
'thousands of children' is my name
tell them again, please, not to shout
let them shout more quietly
let us die more quickly
because he's cold
and we're cold too.

Let's quickly get out of here
and leave alone this man
who weeps and talks
this madman
who could've been you
could've been me
who is none other than us two,
my brother.

*

Halt!
Halt!
Who goes there?

It's no one, buddy
it's merely the world's people:
hungry
tormented
naked
and you're hearing their enraged heart.

And the night patrol officer
will be late
the night patrol officer
won't come
he tried to remember his mother
but couldn't
his mother's face
hidden
behind a black smear

a smear of blood
he slowly opened the door
the depot was dark
he began to feel cold
and hung himself
that he might become warm
rat-a-tat.

What time is it?

*

The stench of burnt metal
the soft sleet
one man crawls
another groans
one man: two holes in the head
another: his legs lie elsewhere.
In the distance a bugle.

In the darkness
their white spats come and go
they step on us to pass through
and the bugle
won't stop
one man: his stomach is red
another: his skin is black
one man plays blind man's bluff
another has no hands.

Cast away
like bundles that have come undone
like bundles of old clothes
on the ground.

At one time they lived.
They'd gaze at the sun
they'd search their pockets for tobacco
and dream of
a different world.
Soon they will be buried.

The smell of urine
blood has its own odour
the stretchers
overturn in the trucks
the dead fall with a heavy thud.
Soon we will forget them.
Such large stretchers
made of thick tarpaulin.

If only one were able to move forward
in the mud
to wait all night
in the rain
but not to be dead
no –
silence!
If only one could die
without ever having lived.
One man has hiccups
another bites a boot
one man exposes his genitals
another doesn't know how to die
and is in agony.

We all gaze at the night
we all have the same night
quietly
the same dream
what dream?
none of us will make it through the night
and that bugle
why does it sound?
give me a moment to search myself
– at home
we had an entire drawer
of safety pins –
to search in case I find one
to bind, my brother
your broken jaw
I would like you to speak to me
we want someone to say to us

'tomorrow'
even to say to us
'never'.
To at least speak to us.

A soldier bends down
hands us his flask
then disappears down the road
in the darkness
one man remembers
another doesn't remember anything
one man has a face of charcoal
another's face is paper.
And that bugle
why doesn't it stop?
why does it sound in the night?
what is it looking for in the night?
Day will break.

But it's still night, comrade
it's freezing, comrade.

*

The major is screaming
he summons the captain
Which lunatic
is sounding the bugle at night?
Onward!
Onward!
the captain calls the sergeant
the sergeant is pale
Onward!
Onward!
The bugler, Captain
was alarmed by the machine guns, Captain
Onward!
Onward!
He's hiding somewhere, Captain
the troops are biting their blankets
the troops are crying, Captain
Onward!

Onward!
the detachment searches in the night
the clouds hang low
it's snowing
Onward!
Onward! …

At a half-demolished outpost
we found him, Captain
a bugler dies easily
how easily we die, Captain
his eyes remained open
just like yours, Captain
but listen
it won't stop
the bugle won't stop
Captain
life won't stop
Onward!
Onward!

Onward!
Onward! …

*

A wall at night
the limestone cracked in many places
separates two cells
separates two men.
One doesn't know the other
yet they recognize each other
just as the executioner lifted his arm
they let out the same cry
just as the day gave way to the night
they both had their hands burnt
just as we shut our eyes for a moment
we all saw the same vision
tomorrow we will reveal it to you.
Their legs broken
their arms twisted
yet they want to pull through

they crawl
the body folds up
then unfolds
like the palm of a hand at one time begging
another time clenched as a fist.

A little longer
the wall is close by
comrade, can you hear me?
he laughs behind the wall
a little tortured laugh
a laugh
like a fissure of light
a laugh that brings death
to those who forget this laughter
comrade, we hear you
this laughter humiliated the enemy.

One doesn't know the other
yet they recognize each other
soon they won't exist
yet they might
their wounded fingers
rouse the wall from sleep
one man says: the sun is for all people
the other says: the day is near
and both say: we will go on.

Beatings in the night
like a child drawing breath
like the cry of a madman
like the steps of a man
coming to meet us
like a heart
a sure heart.

The prison guard has fallen asleep
at the door
the night advances into the night
brothers
my tormented brothers

bend down
put your ear to the wall
to all the walls of the world
to hear these beatings
to hear
your own voice.

The sun is for all people.
The day is near.

We will go on.

THIS STAR IS FOR ALL OF US

For Maria

I

Night came quickly.
The wind came from afar, reeking of rain and war.
The trains hurriedly passed by, full of soldiers
we only just managed to glimpse them through the glass panes.
Great iron helmets barricaded the horizon.
The wet asphalt road glistened. Behind the windows
the women cleaned some dried beans and stayed silent.
And the footsteps of the patrol officer
seized the silence from the road and the warmth from the world.

Turn your eyes towards me so that I may see the sky
give me your hands so that I may hold on to my life.
How pale you are, my beloved!

It seemed someone was knocking on our door at night. Your mother,
dragging her thick wooden sandals, went to open.
No one. No one, she repeated. It must be the wind.
We huddled together. Because we knew
we knew, my beloved, that it wasn't the wind.

Thousands of people were dying outside our door.

See how our neighbourhood has been ruined, my beloved.
The wind enters and exits through the crevices of the houses
the walls are soaked, swollen, then collapse.
Where did so many of our neighbours go without saying goodbye
leaving their stone walls half-whitewashed

their smiles half-finished?
As soon as someone turned the corner we wouldn't see them again.
We'd say 'Good morning' and suddenly night had fallen.

Where are so many children going?
And that blond umbrella vendor who would sing in the morning
executed
and the kiosk owner who would hand us the change with a smile
executed
and the boy who would weigh our coal – remember him?
executed.
His cart overturned in a corner.

Their loved ones will now look at the night straight in the eye
each will bury their head in their beloved's shirt, like a dog, and smell it.

And the postman who would open the windows with his voice
executed.
So take your red lips away from me, Maria.
I'm cold.

Tonight against every wall life is being executed.

My beloved
I love you more than I can say with words
I'd want to die with you, if you were ever to die
and yet, my beloved
I couldn't
I couldn't love you the way I used to.

We closed the door behind us and were cold
we closed the windows and were colder still
and as I turned to look at your eyes
I saw her eyes: the eyes of my neighbour whose four children were killed
and as I reached out to find your hand
it was as though I were stealing bread from the hands of the hungry.

You embraced me
but I was looking over your shoulder at the road.
And when we wanted to talk we suddenly fell silent.
We could hear from afar through the open window

the steps of those condemned to death.
How can our blanket continue to dispel such bitter cold?
How can our door protect us from all this night?
People cast their great shadows amongst us.
What will become of us, my beloved?

My beloved, are you listening?
No, it's not the wind, it comes from far away
you'd think thousands of feet were descending upon the roads
thousands of hobnail boots pounding the asphalt.
Where are they going? How could they be leaving?

How could I live far from you, my beloved?
How could I light a lamp if it wasn't to see you?
How could I look at a wall if your shadow won't pass over it?
How could I lean on a table if your arms won't lean on it?
How could I touch a slice of bread if we won't share it?

But the noise grows louder.
There's nowhere to sleep. No place to sit.
No, it's not the wind, it comes from further back.
Rip up our bedsheet, my beloved
tear up your dress and stop up the crevices.

People hurriedly toss all their belongings into a sack
because their entire belongings are no more than
some bread, a memento and their love of life.
They embrace each other and disappear into the night.

We stay behind. Where do we stay? Why do we stay?
How could I open a door if it wasn't to meet you?
How could I cross a threshold if it wasn't to find you?
No, I couldn't live far from you, my beloved.

But tonight at every corner people await us.
Give me your lips for a moment. And prepare my sack, Maria.

II

It was as though the last memory upon the earth had died.
The wind would blow our tents away

we'd put them up again, only for them to be blown away once more.
The fog walked with a limp over the stones.
Large black barbedwire barricaded the sky.
Night was falling across the entire camp. We wanted to see
but it kept getting darker. The world kept moving further away.
We wanted to listen
but the wind kept blowing. The steps of the sentry kept getting nearer.

Where is the smile that will assure us that we exist?
Where is the voice that will prevent us from getting lost in the night?
We wanted to remember
but we had many dead to bury.

After fatigue duty it was lights out.
And then came the flashlights, the machine guns, the screams
then came fear
we could hear them shouting from the outposts in the night:
Halt!
and our hearts beat faster as they shouted again:
Halt!

You thought you'd die
perhaps you were already dead
such was the night, the rain
the wind
the wounded
when suddenly you sensed a hand fumbling in the dark
and clasping your own hand.

And it was as though the first hope upon the earth was born.

The southerly always drives us mad during the day.
Pales are broken by the wind
– you'd think they were exhumed bones.
We carry large stones from the mountain
we carry on our backs the large grooves made by rifle butt blows
in the evening we sit in the tent and mend our singlets
we say a joke or two
we scoop out with our eyes the bottom of the mess tin.
And we're surprised that our hands have become hard like a heavy
    pair of boots.

The sentry stands outside for a moment and yawns.
Petros smiles as he rips out the lining from his jacket and binds our wounds
old Matt has two calm eyes and three murdered sons
and Elias says: 'I'll find a way to play the harmonica'
that's what Elias says: 'I'll find a way to play the harmonica'
even though they've cut both of his hands.

We change topic.
And you feel that the world isn't large enough for this hole-ridden tent
   to fit into it
yet your heart is large enough for all the world to fit into it.

Thus each night the lamp would wipe away our day.

Thus each day the rain wipes away our steps from the ground.

Whenever they take one of our comrades
we get his clothes ready and give him our hands.
We then place his mess tin to one side.
Night falls.
The empty mess tins quickly multiply in the corner.

One man would like to cough because he doesn't know what to say
another stands for an hour looking at the footprints
left by the shoes of that man
who will never return.

Truly so many comrades
beside the same lamp and the same hope
before the same bread and the same death
when we were cold they cloaked us with their eyes
when we were hungry they apportioned us their heart.
And when we were about to die they spoke to us of life.

Then we too were able to die.

That comrade of ours had a brown beanie
they brought him to us wounded in the evening
when his mother would be lighting the lamp
and the crickets would be singing in the hedges of his hometown.

They had tortured him for days. When we took off his boots
they were full of blood. We sat next to him
without speaking
we ran our fingers through the earth, without speaking
we could only feel our hearts puncturing us
like a fork forgotten in a coat pocket.

It began to rain and we sensed that he would die.
He turned and looked at us. One by one. Farewell Thomas!
And that which your eyes seek from us, we pledge it to you, Thomas.
We will never betray your eyes.

And suddenly in the eyes of our comrade who was departing so simply
I rediscovered your eyes, my beloved.

Yes, my beloved

I could now find you everywhere.
I lit the lamp and trembled, just like when I lit it for you
I shared the bread with my neighbour as though I were sharing it
     with you
and as I reached out to grasp someone's hand, I found your hand
and as I stooped to listen to some voice, I found your voice.

Those who separated us are the same ones now returning you to me.

And I found you in the silence, in a star, in our resolve
in that battered calendar left me by my neighbour before dying
in a flask whose meagre water chirped like your laughter
I found you in our lit cigarettes which glowed in the dark like your tears
I found you in our despair, in our hope, in half a scarf
the other half worn by a comrade the moment he was executed.

I found you again all those nights when I didn't know if I'll see
     you again.
And when in the evening I'd lie down in the freezing tent
and listen to the rain
I would dream
and find you.

I found you, my beloved, in the smile of all the people to come.

III

Yes, my beloved. Long before I met you
I was waiting for you. I was always waiting for you.

When I was a small boy and my mother would see me sad
she'd bend down and ask, 'What's wrong, my child?'
I wouldn't respond. I would only look over her shoulder
at a world bereft of you.
And when I was practicing with a slate pencil
it was to learn how to write you songs.
I would lean against the window when it was raining because you were
    running late
I would gaze at the stars at night because I was missing your eyes
and when there was a thump at my door and I opened it
there was no one there. Somewhere in the world, however, was your
    heart and it was thumping.
That's how I lived. Always.

And when we met for the first time – remember? – you opened your
    arms to me so tenderly
as though you had known me for years. Obviously
you had known me. Because before you came into my life
you had long lived in my dreams,
my beloved.

Do you remember, my love, 'our first big day'?

That yellow dress suited you
a simple and cheap dress, but such a pretty yellow.
Its pockets embroidered with large brown flowers.
The sunshine on your face suited you
the rosy cloud at the end of the road suited you
and that faraway voice of the itinerant tool grinder – it suited you.

I'd put my hands in my pockets, I'd take them out.
We walked without talking. What could one say anyway
when the world is so bright and your eyes so large?
A boy on the street corner was hawking his lemonades.
We shared one between us. And the swallow that suddenly brushed past
    your hair, what did it say to you?
Your hair is so beautiful. It must've said something to you.

In a small hotel, in an old neighbourhood near the station
we saw them through the glare of the sun shunting the trains.

Truly that spring, that morning, that plain room of happiness
your body which I held naked for the first time
the tears which I couldn't hold back in the end
– how they suited you!

Ah, our home was warm back then

our lamp was joyful
the world was vast.
The smell of fried oil emanated from the kitchen.
I bent down, my love, to kiss your flour-coated hands
and my lips were covered in flour. I then kissed you on the mouth
and your lips too were covered in flour.
We looked at each other and laughed.
Spring bade us good evening from the open window. A girl across
   was singing.
How lovely it was to be alive!

Then came the rain. But I wrote your name on all the frosted windows
and so our room was clear and cloudless. I held your hands
and so there were always sky and trust in life.
Do you remember when I'd kneel down in the evening to take off your shoes?
How embittered I was by your shoes! always sorrowful they were and
   worn at the edges
maybe they were even letting in water, my love
but you'd never say anything. You'd only smile.
You'd then silently bend down to mend my old jacket.
Your bowed neck: a blooming almond tree branch.

No, the wind won't take you from my arms
nor will the night
no one will take you. Do you hear? Do you hear?

That was when the days knew nothing of mist
when the sunset would empty an apron full of oleanders into our yard.

Do you remember one evening when I was combing your hair
and you were looking at me in the mirror and softly singing something?

Your hair is as black as a night sky, through your mouth breathes the
    whole of spring
in your hands I laid my heart forever.
Your eyes
ah, what can I say, my love, about your eyes
when your eyes are as beautiful as all the songs of the world put together
when your eyes are as big as the biggest hope.
Your eyes.

Whenever you smiled a dove would fly through our dusk-filled room
a golden cloud would journey through the sky whenever you smiled.
Whenever you smiled I forgot about the leaking roof, I forgot about the
    holes in the floor
I'd even say: look, any moment now
from these holes great red roses will sprout.

Everything was possible in the world, my love
back then
when you smiled at me.

Do you remember that night when we were gazing at the sky for hours?
I felt you trembling in my arms.
'Oh stars,' I said, 'make our love luminous
make my beloved happy.
Oh stars, oh fair stars, see to it that she and I die together.'
And so that night
amongst the stars we were joined forever in wedlock.

Ah, I'd like to kiss your father's hands, also your mother's lap which gave
    birth to you for my sake
and kiss all the chairs you touched with your dress as you passed by
and hide on my breast like an amulet a small piece of the bedsheet you slept in.
I could even smile
at the man who saw you naked before I did
I'd smile at him, seeing that he was granted such limitless joy.
Because I, dear, owe you something more than desire
I owe you song and hope, tears and again hope.

In the briefest moment with you, I lived all of life.

You knew how to surrender yourself, my love. You would surrender
    yourself completely

and you would retain nothing for yourself
other than the worry as to whether you had completely surrendered
	yourself.

As you undressed the leaves in a distant forest rustled
the sky cleared in a flash as you undressed.
Your underwear on the chair: a bouquet of white flowers.
And then nothing else but our love
nothing but you and I
nothing but the two of us
and neither yesterday
nor tomorrow
nothing but the present
nothing but you and I
now, now
together
now together
always together
two together ...

Afterwards I placed the bedsheet on you.
'I'd like our child to take after you,' I said.
'No,' you replied. 'I'd like our child to take after *you*.'

Then they broke down our door.
We had to go our separate ways, Maria,
to separate so that people separate no more.

I placed my hand on your belly to farewell our child.
Goodbye. Goodbye.

Our child, Maria, must take after all the people
who vindicate life.

IV

Night would now be arriving abruptly.
People on the streets would be in a hurry. Women
would be shutting their doors in fear and embracing their children.
But the famished faces of the children cast a black shadow on the wall
like the shadow of bread.

You'd be sitting on that same small stool of ours
the roof always leaking
you'd be stitching the little clothes of our child from an old bedsheet
you'd be patching the emptiness of separation with your bitterness.

I wonder if the sky we gazed at from the window still shines.
Does the small peach tree in the yard continue to blossom?
Workers would be disappearing one by one from the nearby machine shop.

But when there's a knock on our door at night
your mother will no longer be afraid.
She will just light the lamp so that those condemned to death don't lose
    their way
she will then blow on the fire so that the dead keep warm
and you will open the door with sure hands and hear in the night
that loud noise
that relentless marching in the distance.
Because now, dear, you know
because we know.

Thousands of people defend the world
and our love.

Yes, my beloved,
it is for these few and simple things that we fight
so that we might have a door, a star, a stool
a joyful journey in the morning
a peaceful dream at night.
So that we might have a love they can't defile
a song we can sing.

But they break down our doors
they trample upon our love.
Before we begin our song
they kill us.

They're afraid of us and kill us.
They're afraid of the sky we gaze upon
they're afraid of the stone wall we lean upon
they're afraid of our mother's spindle and of our child's primer

they're afraid of your arms that know how to embrace so tenderly
and toil so manly
they're afraid of the words the two of us say in hushed tones
they're afraid of the words all of us together will say tomorrow
they're afraid of us, my love, and when they kill us
as corpses they're afraid of us even more.

I love you more than words can say.
All joy lies in your eyes, the whole of life in your hands
all the world lies on a wall upon which your shadow falls in the evening.
No, I couldn't live far from you, my beloved.

But we know how to love and how to part
this will forever remain ours
this is something no one can take from us.

This love, this war, this faith of ours in life.

Goodbye, then, goodbye.
So that your eyes may always be cheerful
goodbye
so that the beautiful times we had are not forgotten
goodbye
so that the night doesn't frighten us, so that the sky is not stolen from us
goodbye.
So that injustice in the world finally comes to an end
goodbye.

We might even be killed, my love. But who cares?
Thousands of people die every day
without a name
thousands of women woke up in the morning
and suddenly found themselves forever alone.
Children are given neither caress nor bread. Goodbye.

Perhaps I won't return.
Someone else will lock his arms around your warm body.
Don't forget me.
But no, no, my love, you must forget me.
You must completely surrender yourself to him

just as you once surrendered yourself to me.
Only when both of you happen to hear cheering and stand in the middle
    of the road
looking at our flags unfolding in the sun
then
oh, then, remember me – remember me for a moment – one moment only.

And then grab his hand and set out
advancing towards the future.

Come, then, wipe your eyes, don't cry. My God, what beautiful eyes!
Remember when we were sitting one night by the window
in the distance a gramophone was playing and we listened without talking?
You said: 'We might not have a gramophone, and they might not
    have put that record on for us.
But this slow song is ours. And this night is ours.
And that star over there is all ours.' That's what you said.
Taken aback, I replied: 'You speak like a poet, my love.'
You put your lovely arms around my neck
and kissed me. In the way only you know how to kiss.

Come, then, don't cry.
That's the spirit, that's how I like you – smiling.
We will live, my beloved, and we will win. Whatever they do
we will win.

One day we will meet again.
We will then buy a gramophone of our own
and we will have it playing all the time. Yes, my love,
we will even sit by the window, close to one another.

We will meet again one day.
And then
all the nights and all the stars and all the songs
will be ours.

V

I'd like to shout your name, my love, at the top of my voice
so that the builders on the scaffolds hear it and kiss the sun

so that the stokers in ships learn of it and all the roses draw breath
so that spring hears it and arrives more quickly
so that children learn of it and have no fear of the dark
so that it's spoken by the reeds on riverbanks and the turtle doves on fences
so that the world's capitals hear it and repeat it with all their bells
so that it's talked about by washerwomen in the evenings as they massage
    their swollen hands.

I want to shout it so loud
that no dream in the world again sleeps
and no hope any longer dies.
So that time hears it and never touches you, my love.

And see,
it's no longer the two of us within our love.

Within our love my deceased mother ascends a white hill
and gathers in her apron the morning rays
within our love pass all our neighbourhood's murdered children singing
    serenades
within our love all the withered maidens no longer sigh
they too boast a smile, a flower and a young man to whom they will give
    themselves
and that neighbour's mute child is able within our love to sing
within our love a lamp shines upon the humble
within our love a loaf of bread steams up for all the hungry
within our love lies a dewy branch
a sparrow
a harmonica
within our love all the dead are no longer unknown
we call out to them as their mothers did by their first names
within our love thousands of people march with flags
one man falls down, others instantly rush to raise his flag
they are forever marching, forever advancing, forever moving with
    battle cries
– within our love.

And suddenly, my beloved,
it's as though we never parted.
Who could possibly part us two?

Even with this great sea between us
we are near one another
if I were to move ever slightly over the sea
I could touch your hair, I could find your lips.
It's as though we were before an open window
in our home, on a bright May morning.
Look, look, my beloved,
the women of our neighbourhood have come out to whitewash their
    stone walls.
Why are they whitewashing them? They must be waiting for something.
We await too.
Spain awaits too.
Good morning women!

And over there, my love, there in the corner, behold the arrival of spring
behold those young men beckoning us with sickles
and the young women behind them tying the sun's rays in bundles
look, they're beckoning us. Everything beckons us. Good morning!
And those people down there on the horizon, hoisted on a huge
    building site
perhaps they're constructing a new dam or maybe a memorial to our dead.
Perhaps they also want to collect an armful of stars for their lovers.
Good morning!

And there, in the distance, far away
behold that little old woman knitting on a doorstep in Asia.
Do you know what she is knitting, my love? She is knitting for our
    daughter
her future little socks.

Good morning to all you distant brothers of mine!
Come along and I'll introduce you to my beloved. Tell me, isn't she
    beautiful?
I love her, my brothers, like life and like song. Even more so.
Good morning sky! Good morning sun! Good morning spring!
Come, then, and I'll introduce you to my beloved.
Good morning happiness!

And when we die, my beloved, we will not die.
Seeing as people will behold the same star we beheld
seeing as they will sing the song we loved

seeing as they will be drawing breath in a world you and I dreamed up
well then, my love, we will be more alive than ever.

Seeing as people will find us every moment
in peaceful bread
in just hands
in eternal hope
how, my beloved,
could we die?

THE WIND AT THE CROSSROADS
OF THE WORLD

Freezing cold
the wind blows through the deserted city streets
swirling the dust
sweeping along cigarette butts, clouds, papers
some solitary pedestrians hurry through the streets
the wind blows
it blows into the chimneys, in the shelters under the bridges
it blows through the scraggy legs of the prisoners as they drift around
    the courtyard
it blows onto the bleeding bellies of women who give birth outside the
    closed hospital doors
it blows in the slums, in the barracks, in the taverns
it blows beneath the old palace

Requiem for the fallen

Bleachers
ministers' top hats
monocles
gloves
expensive furs
soldiers in file present arms
crowds crammed
behind glistening bayonets

Faces square and wrinkled
faces blue with cold, smudged with smog
thick strong jaws, rotted teeth
eyes beneath crumpled caps
red and sullen

Give rest, O God, unto your servants
hallelujah
the wind blows

An old man half-asleep
a plasterer with overalls covered in lime powder
there's no way out
the Slavs threaten us
the war
quiet! quiet! the minister is speaking
the war
hallelujah
the wind blows through the crutches of the crippled who bang on
    the city doors
it blows through the guitars of the blind who play on street corners
it blows between the bones of the dead

A woman clutches her child in fear
the child is in distress and begins screaming
shut up! the minister is speaking
a bakery worker spits
bastards!
hallelujah
and his spittle, congealed from the flour, expands like leavened dough
to make tomorrow's bountiful bread
take ye, and eat
the wind blows

Workers from the sewers, from the cement factories, from the gasworks
garbage collectors, builders, workers from the abattoirs
women who sell greens at the market
girls who warm their hands under their armpits
huge red hands worn from washing

Our nation is threatened!
For God and country!
We must cut it short, Your Excellency
they're expecting us for tea
where pain shall be no more, nor sorrow
a beggar scratches his crotch

The unknown soldier is cold beneath the fine sleet
an old-timer grinds a chestnut with his toothless gums
a whore hangs from the arm of an American sailor
a girl recollects her childhood prayers
'and peace upon the earth'
the wind blows

The wind blows upon the stretched out, bony hands of beggars on the
      steps of churches
it blows upon the ice-cold, silent queues outside the communal soup
      kitchens
it blows upon the orphanages, the brothels, the children's asylums
it blows
it blows

– We must safeguard the security of the nation
– They say more workers will be sacked tomorrow. What will
      become of us?
– The ermine fur coat suits you marvellously, my dear
– O Christians have mercy upon me, O Christians give me a few pennies
– Blessed be the hungry and the thirsty
– Move away! your breath stinks like a toilet
– The freedom of the fatherland
– I took her to the hospital but they wanted money …
– He's making a call to arms
– She died
– Lighter wicks … Lighter wicks
The wind blows
What will become of us?
Take some, brothers. We also have wicks for dynamite.

Faces furrowed by time and smallpox
faces scarred by hunger and workplace accidents
faces swollen, dirty, hairy
faces pulled by the pincers of a savage smile
faces broad like a mother's breasts
faces hard as anvils

A woman takes out her breast and suckles a pale infant
the wind tangles up the clouds
the clouds are tangled upon the flags

death dons the mask of a general and travels the world
women weep, washing their black clothes
people weep on doorsteps, at street corners, in the fields
they weep in trenches, in hospitals, outside unemployment offices
tears tears
our eyes will live on after our death
so that they may weep
the wind blows

The wind tangles up the voices, the years, the electric cables
it tangles up the teeth of the tobacco worker with the bayonets
it tangles up the minister with a black dog
it tangles up the breast of that woman suckling her baby with the dome
    of the local church
the wind blows

The windowpanes of the great cities are fogged up, sullied by our
    famished breath
as we bury the dead, their mouths remain open
our dead
are hungry

A little girl sits on the doorstep
she has wrapped her father's crutch with a cloth, like a doll
and sings it to sleep
hush little baby, hush

The mansions cast a heavy shadow that breaks our backbone
the roads rush, gasping for breath
the windows are blind
the wind blows

A woman who has given birth howls under the disfigured sky
her husband wanders the streets, begging for a candle
to light beside the baby

Women-gleaners comb the fields
collecting in their aprons bullets, tattered boots and faded letters
ah, mothers give birth give birth
suffer the labour pains
howl from the pains of childbirth

tear up your clothes and wrap up your baby lest it catches a cold
give birth give birth
the war needs more deaths
the wind blows

It blows through the shirts of menial labourers, torn at the elbows
it blows through the holes in the trousers of the jobless
it blows
it blows within the enraged heart of the people

The minister gestures
upon the low black sky
his hands design the betrayal

An old woman crosses herself: Lord of the Powers
– the Powers of the West, of course

A street cleaner shivers from the cold
his teeth chatter
composing a muffled angry song
hey masters!
who shouted?
no one
the wind blows

Those working in vegetable markets, or with bandsaws or with manure
stevedores, washerwomen, quarry workers
crews at ports carrying sacks of flour
80 kilos each
old women cleaning public toilets
their eyes red and swollen from ammonia

The wind roars through the side streets, the town squares, the train
    stations
the roar of shelters, wires, bells
the approaching years roar

Two workers converse in hushed tones
you can't hear what they're saying
you can only see their large lips moving about like arms
ready to strike

A well-polished car pulls up
carrying two bald gentlemen and a fat-arsed woman
the fatherland demands sacrifices

Banks sprawled along the wide pavements
like prehistoric animals digesting their prey

The old woman looks and looks at the unknown soldier standing naked
    in the freezing cold
she takes off her shawl and covers this cold, naked youth

Faces rugged as tree trunks
faces sharp as axes
faces red, copper-green, ashen
faces deep and boundless like the deep and boundless horizon
hands that build the world in an hour
and destroy it in a second
faces rough-hewn, stony, foreboding

A coal worker's eyes against his blackened face
like red emergency lights in the night
one day
we will settle accounts
who shouted?
no one
the wind blows
the war
the war
– tonight we all shouted together

The wind snatches the old woman's shawl
lifts it up high
unfolds it
the shawl grows bigger and bigger
and like a huge black octopus
clutches the city

The wind tangles up the roads, the dates, the faces
it sweeps the dust away from the battlefields
that dust is slowly burying Europe
it blows through the fields, the harbours, the dirt roads

on our windows are reflected the great fires of Asia
a siren screams in the night
SOS
SOS
who is in danger?
it blows through large tunnels where trains pass full of soldiers and
    darkness
where are they going?
SOS
the world is caving in
it blows on the hills, at the crossroads, on the churches
German women sitting on doorsteps sing:

>   Three friends make a start
>   On a journey they set
>   For the Rhine they depart …

the friends were on their way when suddenly
they stumbled upon the war
now they decompose, buried in a foreign land

>   For the Rhine they depart
>   A bit of wine to get …

the wind tangles up gestures, events, blood
it shifts borders and shreds maps
it knocks over the Statue of Liberty and plants in its place an enormous
    wooden cross
it sweeps away clouds, nations, fires
it blows
the wind blows bizarrely tonight, changing the configuration of the world

The soldiers stamp their feet to warm up
sleet slides off their helmets
after the minister a general takes to the podium
Heil Hitler!
oh! my apologies
I meant to say: The Freedom of the Fatherland
the gloves applaud
under the children's shabby overcoats
one can make out pointed, undernourished shoulder blades

A group of girls snickering
at the unzipped pants of a drunkard

The little girl continues to whisper
hush little baby, hush
yet the crutch can't sleep
– it remembers the war
the wind blows

Faces of tar, faces of concrete
thick strong jaws accustomed to not chewing
eyes that cut better than bayonets
their hands are ready to save the world
unto the ages of ages

Quieten down, please
quieten down
you will wake up the dead –
we will wake up
the wind blows upon the scorned and the naked

Someone collapses
who is it? who is it?
two policemen rush
it's nothing it's nothing
a jobless man
fainted
the wind blows
he might even be dead
hallelujah
crossroads like great crosses lying on the ground
bayonets gleam
vanity are all the works of man
pimps
bruised faces
the wind (what will become of us?) blows
hallelujah hallelujah hallelujah

And then there was a great silence.
And the sun began to descend upon the flames of the west.

And the sky turned red. And the ground turned red. Like blood.
And nothing could be heard anywhere on earth.
And gradually from behind the heights
great dark formations could be seen arriving.
From the plains, from the ravines, from the gorges, from the mountains
from all paths they could be seen arriving:
the war dead.

They unfurled in long black files as though they were going to battle.
And they advanced, shuffling their feet and staggering
their bodies bowed, as though they had walked a great distance
as though they had grown tired of waiting so long.
And they advanced hobbling, moving slowly towards the ends of
    the earth.

And every so often the earth trembled, then cracked open
a black-green hand came out of the ground and extended its decayed
    fingers.
The dead stretched themselves and stood upright.
They moved on, stepping upon others who had died
the latter dragging themselves along the ground, grabbing the others'
    greatcoats and drawing themselves up
and the columns joined and multiplied and advanced
the dead in the millions.

And the horizons were lit up red as though the earth were on fire.

They arrived from the trenches, from the underground galleries, from
    the holes
they arrived from the common graves broken open in the plains
there where they had been hurriedly heaped like a shovelled pile of dung.
They arrived with their torn, bloodied greatcoats, covered in a thick
    layer of mud
with eyes glassy and wide open, just as they were the moment they were
    impaled by bayonets
with convulsing mouths, slashed by the last scream.
They arrived from the ashen, deserted battlefields
with faces dirtied and disfigured
for as they fell, others would trample upon them and rush onwards
and all day long boots, wheels and horses would trample upon them
    amidst artillery fire and smoke.

They arrived disembowelled, lacerated, decomposed
breathing with difficulty with inverted heads, and their mouths,
          like wounded holes, gaping open.
And they slowly advanced in the enormous red sunset.

Some held their spilt entrails in their hands
others carried uprooted crosses like rifles on their shoulders
some still had shrapnel lodged in their bones
others were enmeshed in barbedwire, which they had embraced when
     mowed down by machine guns.

From bombarded cities dishevelled women arrived
pressing their dismembered babies against their withered breasts.
And black skeletons charred in the crematoria
their hands burnt and warped, like tree roots, from the agony.

And they gravely advanced, shimmering with thick greasy
     sweat
laughing idiotically, like those who no longer hope for anything
like those who have decided upon something terrible.
And they advanced and twisted and went up and down
and they coiled and multiplied and advanced
make way, make way for the dead!
And the sun descended upon the flames of the twilight.

Where are they going? Where are they going?
Stop them!
the generals gesticulate
the ministers and prostitutes tremble
Stop them!

The top hats tumble
the furs turn back into animals and bite them at the neck
the towering shadow cast by the dead crushes their bones
under that unyielding shadow the officials have huddled
like an accordion that's folding

Soldiers attack!
Officers attack!

All infantry units, all combat units
attack!

The recipients of the Grand Cross drive their teeth into the breasts of
    the generals
whose startled eyes spill onto the asphalt and stir like spiders
How do we kill the dead, Your Excellency?
he-he-he

The soldiers are pale
the weapons in their hands transform into crutches
they then change into candles
they then change
and no longer are there any weapons or soldiers

The dead
            advance
                    speechless
they overturn trucks, they overturn tanks
they trample upon bayonets and bugles

Attack!
he-he-he

A woman screams: my boy!
and falls upon the feet of one of the dead
a quarry worker shouts:
let's join them!
a builder: murderers!
a porter raises his arm
and his huge fist hangs above the mansions
help!
let's join them!
murderers!
my boy! my boy!

And then the wind started up again

The whole crowd stirred and began to advance
a forest of raised fists

an endless clamour
peace
peace

The large clocks in the cities creak as they thrust time forward
builders come down from the scaffolds and advance
those who pave the roads place the mattocks on their shoulders and
    advance
peace
peace

The walls, the houses, the squares, the stations
look in astonishment at that dark multitude
which makes the world shudder
and be reborn
they come from the mines, from the trenches, from the sewers
they come from the depths of time atop steamrollers
listen!
their wheels huff and puff like the breathing of history

Villagers grab their pitchforks and advance
the wind roars through the wheatfields, calves bleat in the yards
pieces of wood and mattocks swirl through the air
the roads, those enormous windpipes of the world,
are strafed with screams
we're coming!
get out of the way!
we make our way down like an avalanche that swells as it
    descends

A boundless fervour from thousands of exhalations
the candles melt all at once at church entrances
the vault of heaven quakes from powerful heart palpitations
we're coming from far away
we're going far away
we marched in mud and blood
we marched over the bones of our children
we marched thousands of years to get here
faces scarred from acid and the fractures of the future
hands which treat sledgehammers and the fate of the world like
    children's toys
peace

The trains whistle
a great roar from all points of the horizon
thousands of hands take hold of the bells and clang them
those with arms missing clutch and pull the ropes with their teeth
women clutch their babies and lift them high like banners
the wind blows their hair
the wind blows and unfurls their hair like flags
we want to sow
we want to weave
we want to give birth
peace
peace

The wind pierces the clouds
and above that ragged mob
there suddenly falls a torrent of light
we are the ones who knead and have no bread
the ones who mine the coal and go cold
we are the ones who have nothing
and we come to take the world
peace
peace
we are the proletarians

Like a flash of lightning tomorrow furrows the capitals
nations broaden as they are elbowed by the crowds
passing shadows fall brusquely like mattocks upon the mansions
that noise is the pulse of a great fever
– you'd think it was the future itself that's marching today

In their darkness, with quivering nostrils
the blind pick up the smell of the rising sun
we are the ones tumbling down from the scaffolding
the ones buried in the mine galleries
the ones screaming as we fall into molten metal
peace
peace
the wind sweeping you away tonight
comes from our breath and our bellows

Thousands of people advance
sullen

rough-hewn
dirty
without any belief in God
bearing like a new gigantic God
their own power
we are the ones crying in all corners of the earth
the ones blaspheming against all the sacred things of the earth
we are the ones singing in all languages of the earth
peace
peace

They advance from all parts of the world
demolishing borders with their thick soles
and with their hard, callused hands laying out on the red horizon
the broad gestures of a new destiny

And behind them comes the wind
behind them comes the great wind
behind them comes the great wind roaring
peace
peace

p e a c e

APPENDIX I
'DON'T TAKE AIM AT MY HEART'[1]

Guard, my brother
guard, my brother
I can hear you walking on the snow
I can hear you coughing in the cold
I know you, brother
and you know me.
I bet you have a photo of a girl in your pocket.
I bet you have a heart in the left side of your chest.

Do you remember?
You used to have an exercise book with sketches of swallows
I used to dream of walking with you side by side
on your forehead a small scar from my slingshot
in my handkerchief I keep your tears wrapped up
your Sunday shoes left behind in the corner of our yard
on the wall of the old house our childhood dreams
written in chalk glimmer still.
Your mother has grown old mopping the stairs of ministry buildings
in the evening she stops at the street corner
and buys some coal from my father's cart
they glance at one another and smile
just as you are loading your gun
and getting ready to kill me.

Your morning eyes have set behind a helmet
you exchanged your childhood hands for a rock-hard rifle
we both hunger for a smile
and a bite of quiet sleep.

---

1. Originally published in Leivaditis, *The Man With the Drum*, 1956.

I now hear your boots on the snow
you will soon go to sleep
goodnight, my sad brother
if you happen to see a bright star it means I'm thinking of you
as you rest your rifle in the corner you will turn once again into a sparrow.

And when they order you to fire
shoot me elsewhere
        don't take aim at my heart.
Somewhere deep within it your childhood face still lives.
I wouldn't want you to wound it.

APPENDIX II
'LITERATURE ON TRIAL'[1]

Last month the poet Tasos Leivaditis was tried in the five-member Court of Appeal for his work *The Wind at the Crossroads of the World* and Andreas Pagkalos for his translation and publication of Stalin's *Economic Problems of Socialism in the USSR.*[2] This trial has deeply moved the broader community because the work of the young poet, Leivaditis, has been widely read and loved by the Greek public. For this reason, many prominent figures in literature and the arts as well as ordinary members of the community hastened to follow the trial and to support the persecuted poet. Four members of the Governing Council of the Society of Greek Writers[3] – Agis Theros, vice-president,[4] and the writers Stratis Doukas,[5] Leon Koukoulas[6] and Christos Levantas[7] – attended the proceedings

1. Originally published in *Epitheorisi Technis* [Greek], vol. 1, no. 3, 25 March 1955, pp. 246– 48; no author given.
2. First published in 1952, shortly before Stalin's death, this small but influential book presents what some regard as the Soviet leader's political and economic testament. Pagkalos' translation was published in 1953. Other works translated by Andreas Pagkalos include: Darwin, *On the Origin of Species*; Freud, *Introduction to Psychoanalysis*; Nabokov, *Lolita*; Gogol, *Taras Bulba*; and as co-translator, Hitler's *Mein Kampf.*
3. Society of Greek Writers (Εταιρία Ελλήνων Λογοτεχνών): established in 1934; previous presidents have included Angelos Sikelianos and Nikos Kazantzakis.
4. Agis Theros (1875–1961): pseudonym of Spyros Theodoropoulos; newspaper publisher, poet and politician, best known for his studies of Greek demotic songs; served in 1957– 59 as president of the Society of Greek Writers.
5. Stratis Doukas (1895–1983): secretary of the Society of Greek Writers from 1953 to 1960; his widely read work, *A Prisoner of War's Story* (first published in 1929), recounts the experiences of an Anatolian Greek who is captured by the Turkish army in the aftermath of the Asia Minor Catastrophe in 1922, but manages to escape to Greece after taking on the identity of a Muslim.
6. Leon Koukoulas (1894–1967): poet, theatre critic and translator, indeed the leading translator of Ibsen's work into Greek; artistic director of the National Theatre from 1937 to 1946; president of the Society of Greek Writers from 1959 till it was shut down by the junta in 1967.
7. Christos Levantas (1904–1975): pseudonym of Kyriakos Chatzidakis; journalist and short story writer.

as witnesses in support of Leivaditis and spoke in the most ardent tones about the peace-loving content of his book, highlighting also the need in our country for freedom of artistic expression. Mr Theros said of Leivaditis' book that it is a 'sublimely lyrical composition full of humanism', and concluded with the observation: 'There is no genuine democracy in Greece'. Subsequently, Mr Doukas noted that 'by isolating particular verses and phrases you could make even the Gospels look like revolutionary texts'. Similarly, Mr Koukoulas and Mr Levantas described the work as a hymn to peace and expressed the desire of all cultured people that an end be brought to the suppression of thought and writing.[8]

However, the most important aspect of the case was the Court's finding in favour of democracy and freedom, acquitting both the poet and the translator, and ordering the restoration of the banned works. In this trial of literature special attention must be drawn to two positive signs. Firstly, the awareness shown by the accused poet of the bearing of his case for the cultural and artistic life of the land, an awareness displayed by the humaneness, dignity and sense of intellectual responsibility with which he invested his defence. Secondly, the address made by the Appeal Court's Prosecutor Mr Laskaris, who in full consciousness of his lofty mission before a literary case of this sort, became the most authentic and fervent voice of a democracy which has suffered yet another blow with the illiberal persecution of a poet.

Mr Leivaditis began his defence by stressing the great significance of the trial, stating: 'I'm on trial for no other offence than that of being a poet'. He continued:

> For this very reason I'd like to briefly discuss the issue of artistic creation, as this I take to be essential to the case before us. Artistic creation is one of the most difficult and complicated manifestations of the human spirit. For a work of art to be created it is not enough that external events be observed by the artist and simply be reproduced by him. Rather, these events which make up what we call 'reality' must be channelled into the artistic consciousness, so as to undergo a multitude of changes and mutations, to undergo a proper fermentation, until this gives birth someday to the artistic emotion which will be the cause and motive for the creation of the work. The book which someone picks up and reads in a single night is one over which its author laboured, suffered, spilled blood and often cried, over a period of years.

---

8. In a newspaper report of the trial ('Freedom of Expression On Trial', *Avghe* [Greek], 10 February 1955), Koukoulas is also said to have drawn a comparison between Leivaditis' book and Irwin Shaw's 1936 anti-war play, 'Bury the Dead', going on to state: 'I haven't seen McCarthy go after Shaw'.

Afterwards, in reference to the content of his book, he stated: 'I sought to illustrate the horrors and miseries piled up by war, to illustrate the tragic experience of two world wars.' He added:

Every war, with the atrocities it perpetrates, the thousands dead it leaves in its wake, the economic disruption it brings, along with moral depravity and psychological upheaval, carries along with it at the same time a powerful anti-war stream which manifests itself at all levels of human activity. And so, together with the thousands of wooden crosses planted in the earth, the last two wars also spread the seeds of a rich flowering of anti-war literature. This anti-war stream isn't a theoretical rejection of war but a natural human reaction to a dangerous situation. It is, one could say, the rising up of the worldwide instinct for self-preservation before the prospect of annihilation and catastrophe.

Having spoken about anti-war writings, he went on to say: 'Amongst these works I aspired to find a place, even a minor one, for my own book.' He then discussed in broad terms the recent crackdown on artistic expression in our country, with the banning of books and the persecution of writers; and he concluded by emphasizing how much a nation has need of art, and in turn how much art has need of freedom in order to fully develop. He further pointed out that from every historical period all that survives are artistic and cultural works, and that the level of civilization in a country accords with its level of artistic freedom. By way of example he brought up ancient Greece, 'whose great artistic masterpieces are owed to freedom of speech and conscience – an ideal which the ancient Greeks placed at the very top of the hierarchy of human values'.

In closing he commented that the ideal of Peace – which is the theme of his book – always constituted one of the most powerful motivating forces in artistic creation. 'Ever since the written word emerged on our planet there has never been an artist who has not dedicated his most creative energies to singing the praises of peace,' he characteristically stated. And he continued:

With this book of mine I too sought to provide my services to Peace. I sought to reveal the thousands of wooden crosses; to reveal the barbedwire, the crematoria, the fear; to reveal the conflagration and death. And along with this, to sing about hope and the future, and people's steadfast resolve to fight for peace. This great problem, one that's very weighty for a young poet, I took up with all the passion and reverence I could muster. My artistic conscience is at ease, for I did my duty as an advocate for Peace. The poet or writer, from the moment they inscribe their first words on paper, is bound by an indissoluble oath to defend the highest values in life: justice, truth, beauty, peace.

And he ended his defence with the following words:

> And so I look to Your Honours not so much for judgement, as for support in the protection of artistic freedom and the preservation of Peace. Finally I'd like to emphasize one more time the great significance of today's trial, as well as my conviction that your verdict will be in favour of artistic freedom in our country and in favour of Peace.

When Leivaditis' defence was over, there soon followed another hymn to the ideal of artistic freedom. This was the speech of the prosecutor, Mr Laskaris.

The prosecutor began by describing the banning of books as 'a most poorly motivated policy' and then made mention of the Constitutions of Greece, all of which, without exception, carry protections for freedom of thought and the press, taking these as forming 'the apex of freedom'; and this 'our nation takes prides in'. He noted that

> prior to the war as well as in recent years books have freely circulated in Greece discussing the plainly revolutionary ideas of Engels, Marx, Lenin, Stalin and others. The Greek state acted rightly in permitting the circulation of these books, as this allows us to learn about these ideas and to go on to refute them or even take them on board and broaden our knowledge.

He went on to say that book bannings invariably had the opposite effect in making the banned authors famous, as had happened with Rhoides[9] and Kazantzakis.[10] He added that the law should only be enforced 'when it has

---

9. Emmanuel Rhoides (1836–1904): author of *Pope Joan*, the only novel he wrote (published in 1866), described by Lawrence Durrell as 'a small masterpiece' (Durrell published an English translation in 1954; a more recent translation, by David Connolly, was published by Aiora Press in 2019). The novel, based upon a medieval legend about a ninth-century female pope, satirized the Catholic Church but was also read as an attack upon the Orthodox Church. The book was anathematized by the Holy Synod of the Orthodox Church of Greece.

10. Nikos Kazantzakis (1883–1957): one of Greece's greatest writers, provoked the ire of both the Catholic and Orthodox churches with his novel *The Last Temptation*, published in 1955. The pope placed the novel on the Index of Forbidden Books, while the Greek Orthodox Church made a concerted effort to ban his books. Upon Kazantzakis' death in October 1957, the Archbishop of Athens refused to allow Kazantzakis' body to lie in state in any church in Athens.

clearly been violated', for 'apart from the obvious cases, it is difficult to discern whether we are dealing with a violation or a mere critique'.

'When a book clearly aims at inciting citizens to violently overthrow the government, then the law may be applied and the book banned.' Stalin's *Economic Problems of Socialism in the USSR* was described by the prosecutor as a work of economics, a scientific study, which is circulating freely in all parts of the world and which cannot be labelled 'seditious'. As for Leivaditis' book, he stated that he has read it and found that 99 per cent of its content was in praise of peace; the book's purposes he thought were 'impressive'. The prosecutor went on to condemn wars of aggression, but observed that there are wars that are just, such as those motivated by self-defence and liberation. 'These latter kinds of war are waged by all nations,' he continued. 'Indeed, the fatherland of contemporary communism defended itself heroically against its invaders; we too fought against the aggressor, just as in 1821 we fought for freedom.'[11]

The prosecutor then pointed out that the ideological outlook of any given citizen, or whether or not they subscribe to communism, does not come within the purview of the criminal law, as ideas are not punishable. He also made reference to the 'suspicion' provoked by the 'source' of the peace movement, given that 'that country[12] continues to accumulate arms'. But he added that 'social degradation is something that all writers testify to'; what counts is that 'people's misery is not exploited for ideological reasons'. He concluded by demanding the acquittal of both of the accused.

The prosecutor's speech greatly satisfied the packed courtroom. And that afternoon, after a brief deliberation, the court acquitted the accused men and ordered the restoration of the banned books. This occasioned the most laudatory commentary within the literary circles of the capital. These circles stressed that the court's verdict must put an end once and for all to the intolerable predicament within which our writers have been placed.

The trial was reported by the daily press. *Ta Nea* newspaper,[13] in its lead article of 11 February, headed 'The Banning of Books', focused upon the following comment made by the Prosecutor: 'The banning of books contravenes the democratic traditions of our nation.' 'Such outspokenness,' the newspaper stated, 'was to the Prosecutor's credit, and by extension to the

---

11. For this reason, according to the prosecutor, Leivaditis was not entirely justified in condemning all wars. This comment made by the prosecutor was not included in the above *Epitheorisi Technis* article, though it can be found in the report of the court case in the February 10 edition of the newspaper *Avghe*.
12. The reference, no doubt, is to the Soviet Union.
13. *Ta Nea* (Τα Νέα) is a daily newspaper, published in Athens since 1931.

credit of Greece's justice system [...] It was necessary for this to be said, particularly in a Greek court, and indeed to be proclaimed aloud.'

Mr Psathas[14], in his column in *Ta Nea*, offers a most lively analysis of book bannings in light of the Appeal Court trial, and responds thus to the acquittal: 'Thank goodness! This sorry affair of book bannings and the persecution of writers and publishers has lately gone too far.' And he concludes: 'This verdict ought to function from here on as a benchmark for those in power who have become a law unto themselves.'

---

14. Dimitris Psathas (1907–1979): popular satirist and playwright, also long-standing court reporter and columnist for *Ta Nea*. In the article quoted from here (published in *Ta Nea* on 11 February 1955), Psathas points out that books by Hugo, Balzac, Dostoevsky and Gorky had also recently been banned, and that leftist Greek writers have been exiled to island prison camps. One such Greek writer singled out by Psathas is Menelaos Lountemis (1912–1977), a popular and prolific author, who after several years in island prison camps was brought to trial in 1956 for writing an allegedly seditious short story; the court ordered that all his books be taken out of circulation.

CPSIA information can be obtained
at www.ICGtesting.com
Printed in the USA
JSHW051918211122
33586JS00001B/13